Heavenly
HYDRANGEAS

A Practical Guide for the Home Gardener
— JOAN HARRISON —

Schiffer
Publishing Ltd
4880 Lower Valley Road • Atglen, PA 19310

Copyright © 2013 by Joan Harrison
Library of Congress
Control Number: 2012956333

Designed by Justin Watkinson
Cover by John Cheek
Type set in BauerBodni BT/Zurich BT

ISBN: 978-0-7643-4419-0
Printed in China

Published by Schiffer Publishing, Ltd.
4880 Lower Valley Road
Atglen, PA 19310
Phone: (610) 593-1777
Fax: (610) 593-2002
E-mail: Info@schifferbooks.com

For the largest selection of fine reference books on this and related subjects, please visit our website at
www.schifferbooks.com.
You may also write for a free catalog.

This book may be purchased from the publisher. Please try your bookstore first.

We are always looking for people to write books on new and related subjects. If you have an idea for a book, please contact us at proposals@schifferbooks.com

Schiffer Books are available at special discounts for bulk purchases for sales promotions or premiums. Special editions, including personalized covers, corporate imprints, and excerpts can be created in large quantities for special needs. For more information contact the publisher.

In Europe, Schiffer books are distributed by
Bushwood Books
6 Marksbury Ave.
Kew Gardens
Surrey TW9 4JF England
Phone: 44 (0) 20 8392 8585
Fax: 44 (0) 20 8392 9876
E-mail: info@bushwoodbooks.co.uk
Website: www.bushwoodbooks.co.uk

Some hydrangea varieties mentioned in this book have trademarked or registered names. They include Abracadabra™ Hydrangea Series, Cityline™ Series, Dutch Ladies™ Series, Edgy™ Hydrangea Series, Endless Summer® Collection, Forever & Ever® Series, Halo Hydrangeas™ Series, Bella Anna®, Incrediball™, Invincibelle® Spirit, White Dome™, Angel Eyes™, Angel Lace™, Angel Robe™, Angel Smile™, Angel Song™, Angel Star™, Angel Wings™, 'Blushing Bride' (Endless Summer® series), Cityline™ Berlin, Cityline™ Mars, Cityline™ Paris, Cityline™ Rio, Cityline™ Venice, Cityline™ Vienna, Endless Summer®, Forever & Ever® Blue Heaven, Forever & Ever® Double Pink, Forever & Ever® Fantasia, Forever & Ever® Hydrangea, Forever & Ever® Peace Hydrangea, Forever & Ever® Peppermint, Forever & Ever® Pistachio, Forever & Ever® Red Hydrangea, Forever & Ever® Summer Lace, Forever & Ever® Together, Forever & Ever® White Out, Halo Hydrangeas™ series, Let's Dance® Big Easy, Let's Dance® Moonlight, Let's Dance® Starlight, Mini Penny™, Pink Elf®, Pink Shira™, Princess Lace®, Queen of Pearls®, Sabrina™, Sandra™, Selina™, Shakira™, Sharona™, Sheila™, Sonja™, Soroya™, Stella™, Twist-n-Shout®, Little Lime™, Pink Diamond™, Pinky Winky™, White Diamonds™, Kaleidoscope® Series (a.k.a. Hovaria® Series), Let's Dance® Hydrangea Series, and Royal Majestics® Series. Their use herein is for identification purposes only. All rights are reserved by their respective owners.

The text and products pictured in this book are from the collection of the author of this book, its publisher, or various private collectors. This book is not sponsored, endorsed or otherwise affiliated with any of the companies whose products are represented herein. They include Abracadabra™ Hydrangea Series, Cityline™ Series, Dutch Ladies™ Series, Edgy™ Hydrangea Series, Endless Summer® Collection, Forever & Ever® Series, Halo Hydrangeas™ Series, Bella Anna®, Incrediball™, Invincibelle® Spirit, White Dome™, Angel Eyes™, Angel Lace™, Angel Robe™, Angel Smile™, Angel Song™, Angel Star™, Angel Wings™, 'Blushing Bride' (Endless Summer® series), Cityline™ Berlin, Cityline™ Mars, Cityline™ Paris, Cityline™ Rio, Cityline™ Venice, Cityline™ Vienna, Endless Summer®, Forever & Ever® Blue Heaven, Forever & Ever® Double Pink, Forever & Ever® Fantasia, Forever & Ever® Hydrangea, Forever & Ever® Peace Hydrangea, Forever & Ever® Peppermint, Forever & Ever® Pistachio, Forever & Ever® Red Hydrangea, Forever & Ever® Summer Lace, Forever & Ever® Together, Forever & Ever® White Out, Halo Hydrangeas™ series, Let's Dance® Big Easy, Let's Dance® Moonlight, Let's Dance® Starlight, Mini Penny™, Pink Elf®, Pink Shira™, Princess Lace®, Queen of Pearls®, Sabrina™, Sandra™, Selina™, Shakira™, Sharona™, Sheila™, Sonja™, Soroya™, Stella™, Twist-n-Shout®, Little Lime™, Pink Diamond™, Pinky Winky™, White Diamonds™, Kaleidoscope® Series (a.k.a. Hovaria® Series), Let's Dance® Hydrangea Series, and Royal Majestics® Series among others. This book is derived from the author's independent research.

FOR Mom, Maureen, Barbara, Christopher, and Gregory, and in loving memory of Dad and Dan. Lucky am I to have such a nurturing family.

FOR Caroline, Paul, and Charlotte.
You bring so much happiness into my life.

FOR John. With love.

Contents

Acknowledgments

The beauty of hydrangeas must be contagious. It has been my experience that people who love hydrangeas are beautiful people. They are generous with information and advice, they open their gardens and conduct personalized tours, they freely offer cuttings, bouquets of fresh flowers and sometimes entire plants, and they do this with warmth and good cheer. I am always happy in the company of fellow lovers of hydrangeas.

Members of the Cape Cod Hydrangea Society have enhanced my life. Thank you, all of you, for helping to create a society with its priorities straight as we learn about hydrangeas in an atmosphere of friendship and camaraderie. Special thanks to Joy Bogstad, Joan Brazeau, Judy Deal, Rita Drogo, Betty Hann, Nancy Larned, Elizabeth Payne, Carol Swirbalus, and Mary Anne Tessier. The successful launch of our hydrangea society can be traced directly back to your contributions. Mal and Mary Kay Condon provided the perfect destination for our first field trips. We were just a ferry ride away from their wonderful Hydrangea Farm Nursery on Nantucket. I will always be grateful for your warm hospitality, encouragement, and support. You have helped to make the Cape Cod Hydrangea Society the vital organization it is today.

I have been passionate about learning all I can about hydrangeas. Certain people along the way have been particularly helpful with information and answers to questions, especially Michael Dirr, Glyn Church, Mal Condon, Frank Dutra, Luc Balemans, Eddie Aldridge, Ozzie Johnson, Kristin Van Hoose, and Corinne and Robert Mallet.

In 1990, Susie Simon brought me a hydrangea as a housewarming gift, thus launching a passion for hydrangeas that has changed my life. I can never thank Susie enough for her friendship and inspired gift.

Special thanks to my family and friends for all you do to make me feel loved and supported. I am lucky to have each and every one of you in my life.

HOW TO BEGIN THE SELECTION PROCESS

1

Putting the Right Plant in the Right Place

Hydrangeas have surged in popularity in recent years as home gardeners have learned to appreciate their many positive attributes, especially the long period of bloom combined with ease of maintenance. Plant breeders are introducing new varieties every year so that what was a fairly simple selection process has now become more complicated. While having many more beautiful hydrangea varieties to choose from is quite a positive development, selecting from among them can sometimes feel confusing. People approach the task differently depending on their priorities, but the common goal for all is to put the right plant in the right place.

What is "the right plant"? It is the plant that satisfies some need of the gardener making the choice. It is, moreover, a plant that performs well in the garden's climate. It blooms at the desired time of year and the color of the blooms coordinates well with those of existing plants in the same area. "The right place" will allow the plant to grow comfortably to its mature size without impinging on other plants or causing navigation problems in the garden due to excessive spread. It will not block desired views from windows and it will be situated to catch just the right amount of sunlight. If you take the time to make careful selections, those plants will provide you with years of enjoyment and no regrets.

Many gardeners are attracted to mopheads with their eye-catching colors. Here, purple and blue mopheads create a satisfying color combination.

Different sun and shade conditions determine the best choice for a particular garden area. The white flowers in the foreground are a variety called 'Annabelle', a popular choice from the arborescens species known to do well in full sun on Cape Cod where this picture was taken. Mopheads were chosen for the area closer to the house to take advantage of the recommended protection from afternoon sun.

Species

Because the choice of plant is so important to the gardener's ultimate satisfaction, several chapters are dedicated to help with the selection process. Start by asking yourself why you want to add one or more hydrangeas to your garden. Is it because you saw one in your neighbor's garden and you want the same variety? Was your eye caught by a certain color hydrangea and you want that same color in your garden? Did you see a friend's dried hydrangea wreath that makes you want some of your own hydrangeas that dry well? Are you looking for low maintenance plants in general and have heard that hydrangeas are easy to care for? Did you see a display of hydrangeas that took your breath away and you want to create a similar display in your own garden? Whatever your starting point, the following chapters will guide you toward the right plant or plants to satisfy your requirements.

If you are aware of only blue, pink, and white hydrangeas with their distinctive round flower heads, you may be surprised to learn about the other species available to the home gardener. Chapter Two is devoted to hydrangea species and will fill you in on the five species most commonly available at garden centers. Before you make a choice it is helpful to know the full range of plant materials available to you.

Mophead and lacecap hydrangea flowers can change color depending on the pH of the soil. The variety shown here is 'Alpenglühen' with flowers that tend to stay pink even in an acidic soil, perfect for a gardener who loves pink flowers but who lives in an area where blue flowers are more common.

Climate

Naturally you want to make sure the plant suits your climate. Some hydrangeas are hardier than others and this could be an important factor depending on where you live. Chapter Three deals with climate issues including USDA Hardiness Zones and the concept of microclimates.

Size

Hydrangeas lined up at a garden center in their plastic pots might be temporarily identical in size which makes it easy to forget their mature size. A good plant label will reveal the usual height and spread of the plants, but not all plants are well labeled. Before you go to the garden center it makes good sense to have a general idea of how big the hydrangeas you have in mind

are likely to get. Chapter Four helps you anticipate growth to allow for the space needed by the different species and the size range within a species.

Sun/Shade

Just as you need to consider your climate when making selections, you need to think about the amount of sunlight required by plants in order to thrive. Putting a sun-loving plant in

If you go to a garden center expecting a simple choice, you might feel overwhelmed. A good garden center offers a wide range of cultivars representing several different species. Narrowing your search before you go can help make the selection process less confusing. *Photo taken at Country Garden, Hyannis, Massachusetts.*

the shade or a shade-loving plant in full sun can only lead to plant stress and gardener frustration. Chapter Five outlines the sun and shade requirements of different hydrangea species including both the amount of sunlight needed and the time of day when sunlight is most desired.

Color

Flower color is often the primary consideration when selecting hydrangea varieties. Hydrangea flower colors can be particularly challenging when you have seen the color you want, but you don't know the name of the variety. Hydrangeas have the chameleon-like tendency to change color based on soil composition which confuses the issue further. Chapter Six clears up color mysteries and makes recommendations for the best blues, pinks, purples, and whites.

Traits

Home gardeners frequently seek out plants with specific characteristics. A flower arranger desires plants that yield good cut flowers. Someone who lives near the ocean focuses on plants that can tolerate seaside conditions. A rooftop gardener wants plants that do well in containers. Chapter Seven makes recommendations about hydrangeas with specific traits, including good cut flowers, good dried flowers, hydrangeas good for containers, hydrangeas that tend to rebloom after the first flush of blooming, hydrangeas with large flower heads, and hydrangeas good for seaside locations.

Take note of what appeals to you

The need to seek out certain hydrangeas is often triggered by seeing something appealing in someone else's garden. You may have seen this garden in person, or you read about a garden featured in a magazine article or gardening book. It really doesn't matter where you saw it as the end result is the same; you want to create a similar look in your own garden. If the garden appeared in a magazine or book you can save the pages to have with you when you visit the garden center. If you see a garden in person, try to take pictures, if allowed, or draw as detailed a sketch as possible as soon as you can while it is still fresh in your memory. Visual aids are extremely helpful when it comes to garden design.

Hydrangea flowers can be blue, pink, white, purple, or green. The flower heads can be small, medium, or large. Choosing the desired color and size of flower is a good start toward making a satisfying selection.

HOW TO SELECT HYDRANGEAS BY SPECIES

2

Differentiating the Popular Species

Choosing the perfect plant for a specific location in your garden is rarely accomplished on impulse. The odds are improved when you spend some time thinking about the characteristics of the ideal plant for that spot. Should it be short or tall? What color flowers do you have in mind? When would you want it to be in bloom? How would it look with nearby plants? The more questions you ask and answer, the more successful your selection is likely to be.

The world of hydrangeas offers an ever-increasing selection of wonderful plants for the home gardener. When hydrangeas are mentioned most people picture mopheads with their great big (often blue) rounded flower heads that can't be missed in the garden, but there are other hydrangeas to consider. Lacecaps are becoming increasingly popular as gardeners get better acquainted with them. Some people declare that every garden should be graced with *Hydrangea arborescens* 'Annabelle' and, indeed, a cluster of Annabelles with their big white pompom-like flowers can provide big impact. Then there are paniculatas, oakleafs, and climbing hydrangeas, all with assets to be weighed along with the others. One of the goals of this chapter is to acquaint you with the wide range of hydrangea species and cultivars available so that you can make well-informed decisions.

It may surprise you to learn there are more than twelve hundred hydrangea varieties from which to choose, but don't let that fact overwhelm you. It is relatively easy to narrow the range once you identify what you want. The key is to identify the characteristics you are looking for. Do you want a hydrangea with deep blue blossoms? A small hydrangea for a patio container? A hydrangea with flowers that dry well? A tall sturdy hydrangea to serve as a hedge? A hydrangea that will tolerate full sun? A delicate lacecap hydrangea with pink flowers? All of these characteristics (and more) are present in the range of **species** and **varieties** currently available to the home gardener.

Species and Varieties

All plants eventually end up in botanical categories, with some categories more general than others. Mopheads and lacecaps make up the species called *Hydrangea macrophylla*. The word "macrophylla" simply means big-leafed. Botanists noticed that a large group of hydrangeas had big leaves and placed them all together in the same category. Within the macrophylla species there are two distinctly different flower shapes: mopheads and lacecaps. These are further divided into varieties with individual traits. For example, some are early bloomers. Some are more sun tolerant than others. Some have exceptionally large flowers. Other possible traits include sturdy stems, a rounded form, a small size, and abundant flowering and this is by no means an exhaustive list.

The leaves on mophead and lacecap shrubs tend to be quite large which is the reason for their botanical name "macrophylla" which means *big leaf*.

Popular Hydrangea Species

The following are the species covered in this book, chosen because they are in demand and therefore most commonly available at local garden centers.

Hydrangea macrophylla
  (mopheads and lacecaps)
Hydrangea paniculata
  (panicle hydrangeas including the well known 'Pee Gee')
Hydrangea arborescens
  (smooth leaf hydrangea including the popular 'Annabelle')
Hydrangea quercifolia
  (oakleaf hydrangea)
Hydrangea petiolaris
  (climbing hydrangea)

This blue mophead is the variety called 'Amethyst'.

'Fasan' is an example of the lacecap form of *Hydrangea macrophylla.* \

A plant's habit (characteristic appearance) becomes obvious when you see the plant at maturity. Not all mopheads are mounded and covered with flowers as this one is. It is a good idea to read plant labels for information about the plant's habit.

Mopheads and Lacecaps
(*Hydrangea macrophylla*)

Mopheads and lacecaps thrive under the same conditions. They both prefer morning sun and afternoon shade in a rich moist soil with good drainage. Each type offers flowers in a similar range of colors: blue, pink, purple, and white. When choosing between mopheads and lacecaps (if you must), there are some differences you should take into consideration.

A lacecap shrub with abundant flowers.

BLOOM TIME

Lacecaps tend to bloom earlier in the season than mopheads. For instance, Cape Cod gardeners will see their lacecaps blooming in June with the mopheads coming into full flower in July and August. While the lacecap blooms may last for several weeks, their overall bloom time tends to be shorter than for the mopheads.

DRYING POTENTIAL

If you plan to dry the flowers eventually, please note that mopheads are better for that purpose. This is not to say you can't dry lacecaps successfully – you can, depending on the variety – but it would take considerably more dried lacecaps to create a similar strong impact achieved with just a few mophead flowers. On the other hand, if the effect you want to achieve is very delicate, lacecaps might be the

perfect choice. Lacecaps have an interesting quirk when blooms are fading and they are ready to harvest for drying; the sterile flowers (along the outer rim) turn upside down. This can be good news or bad news depending on the look you are trying to achieve with dried flowers.

GARDEN CENTER AVAILABILITY

Local garden centers tend to stock more mopheads than lacecaps, in response to consumer demand, although the supply of lacecap varieties is steadily increasing as gardeners become more aware of their beauty.

Panicle Hydrangeas
(*Hydrangea paniculata*)

The author first fell in love with paniculatas during a trip to Deerfield, Massachusetts, where masses of Pee Gees were spotted as a tall hedge dividing two residential properties. The common name of this variety, *Pee Gee,* is derived from the first letters of its botanical name, *paniculata* 'Grandiflora'. Its flower heads are cone-shaped panicles (*paniculata*) and tend to be quite large (*Grandiflora*). The species is paniculata; this variety is called 'Grandiflora'. Many of the varieties in the paniculata species have flowers that bloom first

Paniculatas in France showing abundant flowering in mid-August.

Hydrangea paniculata 'Limelight' at the entrance of Heritage Museums and Gardens in Sandwich, Massachusetts.

A paniculata hydrangea trained as a small tree.

white, then cream (for most of the growing season), then pale pink in the fall, eventually deepening to a rich burgundy.

Paniculatas come into their season just as the mopheads are fading away. The plants overall are larger than the mopheads and the lacecaps, thus providing big impact in the late summer/fall garden. They function well as stand-alone specimen plants or massed into large clusters. They make beautiful hedges, with continuous color from early August well into October.

Anyone desiring hydrangeas as a source of dried flowers should try to plant at least one paniculata in their garden. Not only do the flowers dry beautifully; they can also, depending on when they are harvested, yield a richly textured arrangement in tones of cream, pink, and burgundy.

Paniculatas can be trained as trees and, as such, make beautiful specimen plants. They do well in full sun, including the intense afternoon sun that often wilts the mopheads and lacecaps.

They bloom on new wood (wood that has grown that year) so there is no fear about early spring frosts damaging emerging buds. If you don't want to worry about winter protection, this is a good species to consider.

Smooth Leaf Hydrangeas
(*Hydrangea arborescens*)

This hydrangea species is sometimes referred to as a wild hydrangea since it thrives in woodland settings. It is known for its big white "snowball" flowers that can be used with dramatic effect. The variety needs to be chosen carefully because some of the members of this species tend to flop over rather easily due to their sometimes enormous flower heads. As the plants mature the stems become stronger and more able to support the heavy blooms.

Like the paniculatas they bloom on new wood (i.e., the current season's growth). They can be cut back severely in the spring and still

Hydrangea arborescens 'Annabelle' in Chatham, Massachusetts. The flowers of this plant in early July retain a greenish cast before they turn pure white.

A Nantucket display of *Hydrangea macrophylla* 'Annabelle'. Note that this variety grows well in both sun and shade in the Cape Cod region but would not do as well in full sun in the South.

Hydrangea arborescens 'Hayes Starburst'.

put on a glorious show of flowers in summer and fall. The best known variety is 'Annabelle'.

The flowers of *Hydrangea arborescens* 'Annabelle' are green when they first appear in the spring. By mid-summer they are completely white. The aging process causes them to revert to green and these do well as both cut flowers and dried flowers.

The amount of sun this species tolerates depends on geography; the further north the garden, the greater the acceptable exposure to the sun. It is commonly found in woodland areas in southeastern United States, but further north, on Cape Cod in Massachusetts, it can be planted in full sun. If you plan to dry the flowers eventually, you would be well advised to plant it in dappled shade. It is more forgiving than some of the other hydrangea

Hydrangea arborescens 'Invincibelle™ Spirit' in front of 'Annabelle'.

species, as it is resistant to drought and tolerant of severe cold.

'Annabelle' is clearly the best known and most widely planted variety in the species, but there are many others worthy of a spot in the home garden including 'Hayes Starburst', 'Green Knight', White Dome™ ('Dardom'), and 'Wesser Falls'. Recently some pink Annabelles have been introduced to the gardening world, including Invincibelle® Spirit and Bella Anna®.

The various *Hydrangea arborescens* cultivars have many landscaping uses as they are very attractive on their own and also combine well with many other plants.

Oakleaf Hydrangeas
(*Hydrangea quercifolia*)

The foliage on these hydrangeas quite noticeably resembles oak leaves; hence the common name of this plant. The flowers at the height of their season are white or cream and more cone-shaped (like the paniculatas) than round (like the mopheads).

The leaves provide rich fall color and some varieties have exfoliating bark, providing winter interest. This plant tolerates full sun and makes both an attractive specimen plant and a good choice for combining with others for autumn texture. It is a native of the

Hydrangea quercifolia 'Alice' in a Cape Cod garden.

Beautiful double flowers on *Hydrangea quercifolia* 'Snowflake'.

A climbing hydrangea in bloom in mid-June. South Yarmouth, Massachusetts. A younger climbing hydrangea has been planted at the base of the other tree supporting the hammock.

Helpful sign explaining botanical names at J.C. Raulston Arboretum in Raleigh, North Carolina.

southeastern United States and, as such, is quite heat-tolerant. In fact, it seems to flower best in high heat conditions.

Similar to paniculatas, the oakleafs (depending on the variety) go through color changes from one season to the next; white (or creamy white) flowers appear in summer and gradually turn pink in the fall. The pink flowers deepen to burgundy and eventually turn a rich, chocolate-brown.

The flowers dry well if harvested in the fall. If you want to dry them in the burgundy stage, pay close attention to them. You may have a very short window of opportunity before they turn brown, sometimes less than a week.

Climbing Hydrangea
(*Hydrangea petiolaris*)

The climbing hydrangea, splendid at full maturity, is not for gardeners who desire instant gratification. Indeed, for an entire growing season it can give the impression of a plant that doesn't have a clue about how to climb. A climbing hydrangea planted in the spring at the base of a tree may look healthy, but will not appear to grow at all that first season. The following year it will grow only slightly, starting to attach itself to the base of the tree. The third year it will creep a little further up the tree to about four feet above the ground. At this rate, you may imagine it will take forever to reach the top of the tree. The fourth year, however, is when it really starts to take off, scrambling with wild abandon up the trunk of the tree like a child on the first day of summer vacation.

Climbing hydrangeas used to cover a privacy fence in Harwich, Massachusetts.

Climbing hydrangeas make excellent vertical elements in this courtyard garden in Plymouth, Massachusetts.

A shed in Harwich, Massachusetts, is topped with climbing hydrangeas in early June.

This is typical of the growth pattern of climbing hydrangeas. There are many plants that follow this pattern. You may have heard the expression: *First it sleeps, then it creeps, and finally it leaps.* The reality is that for its first few years the climbing hydrangea has to be busy growing below ground where you can't see the progress as it expands and strengthens its roots. The information label provided at the garden center will often indicate this with the words: "Slow to get established".

The plant itself is strong and sturdy but its flowers are delicate. They are white or cream-colored with flower heads resembling those of lacecap hydrangeas. The flowers generally don't appear until the hydrangea has completed its climb on whatever support it is using, so the shorter the support, the faster the flowering. Think of the primary growth as the attachment phase, when the hydrangea is climbing its support. The secondary growth is the flowering phase, when there is some branching out from where the plant is attached to its support. If you want flowers sooner rather than later, you'd be wise to plant your climbing hydrangea at the base of a six-foot trellis rather than a forty-foot tree. While the primary growth is climbing up that tall tree, some secondary growth can appear at the lower levels but flowering will be sparse until the hydrangea reaches the top of the tree. The

Climbing hydrangeas bloom in early spring. This climbing hydrangea traveled up a light pole where the white flowers complement the rich color of the rhododendron blooms.

A climbing hydrangea on the side of a Nantucket house in mid-June.

author planted a climbing hydrangea at the base of a tall oak tree and waited six years before the first flower appeared, and it was the only flower that appeared that season. The following year there were six flowers. More flowers are expected every year but a real profusion of flowers isn't likely to occur until the plant finishes its climb.

If you want to cover a six-foot structure fairly quickly, like a trellis or a fence surrounding an outdoor shower, plant several climbing hydrangeas along the base about three feet apart. Entertain yourself by betting which plant will be the first to reach the top.

Climbing hydrangeas tolerate poor soil (as long as it has good drainage), grow well in either sun or shade, and are very low-maintenance. They cling to any rough-textured surface. Stone walls and trees with rough bark are ideal. Whatever structure is used should be quite substantial since the mature climber can become quite heavy.

The climbing hydrangea is the only hydrangea species also suitable as a ground cover. If you have to deal with a steep slope, consider putting in a few of these plants and in a few years the slope will be covered completely. When you notice tendrils of a climbing hydrangea planted at the base of a trellis or tree start to creep away from the base, take advantage of this situation by cutting them off from the parent plant and placing them in a new desired location. The author planted a climbing hydrangea at the base of a tree supporting a hammock. The goal, very definitely in the delayed gratification department, was to have a profusely flowering climbing hydrangea to admire from the relaxed vantage point of the hammock. Several tendrils of the plant had managed to creep about a foot away from the base of the tree before their attempted escape was noticed. A garden spade was fetched and a quick jab cut the tendrils from the established plant. Almost zero effort was then required to lift the escaping tendrils onto the spade and ferry them over to the base of the other tree supporting the hammock. There they were gently firmed into place and watered well. Several additional years will be required for those tendrils to scramble up that tree but think of the reward: a profusion of climbing hydrangea flowers visible from each end of the hammock.

Award Winning Hydrangea Cultivars

The Royal Horticultural Society in England bestows their Award of Garden Merit (AGM) on plants that are reasonably easy to grow, excellent for garden decoration, of good constitution, essentially stable in form and color, and are reasonably resistant to pests and diseases. All of the following award winners are recommended for home gardens.

Mopheads: 'Altona'; 'Ami Pasquier'; 'Europa'; 'Générale Vicomtesse de Vibraye'; 'Madame Emile Mouillère'; 'Nigra'; 'Parzifal'; 'Preziosa'; and 'Westfalen'.

Lacecaps: 'Blue Wave' (a.k.a. 'Mariesii Perfecta'); 'Geoffrey Chadbund' (a.k.a. 'Möwe'); 'Lanarth White'; 'Lilacina'; 'Tokyo Delight'; 'Veitchii'; and 'White Wave' (a.k.a. 'Mariesii Grandiflora').

Arborescens: 'Annabelle'; and 'Grandiflora'.

Paniculatas: 'Big Ben'; 'Dolly'; 'Kyushu'; 'Limelight'; 'Phantom'; Pink Diamond™; 'Pink Lady'; Pinky Winky™; and 'Silver Dollar'.

Choosing the Right Species for your Needs

It is always wise to decide which plant characteristics are most important to you and start with those when attempting to make good selections. The following tables are designed to help point you in the right direction.

COLOR

Flower color	Species
Blue/purple	macrophylla
Pink	macrophylla, paniculata, quercifolia, arborescens
White/cream	all
Green	macrophylla, arborescens

SUN AND SHADE REQUIREMENTS

As a general note, hydrangeas can take more sun in moist climates such as those found in maritime conditions, and less in hot, dry climates where plants can dry out too quickly and flowers become scorched. The further south the location, the more shade is recommended. When in doubt try for morning sun and afternoon shade.

Sun/shade	Species
Full sun	all, especially paniculata and quercifolia
Partial sun	all
Shade	arborescens, quercifolia

SPECIAL CONDITIONS

Gardeners who live close to the ocean know that some plants thrive under the wind and moisture conditions that prevail while many struggle. The wise gardener chooses plants that not only survive but thrive in these conditions. Similarly, gardeners who live in an area prone to drought are wise to choose plants based on their tolerance of these conditions. The table below suggests good choices in the hydrangea family based on these special gardening conditions.

Special Conditions	Species
Seaside	macrophylla
Shade	arborescens, paniculata

HARDINESS

The zones listed below refer to USDA Plant Hardiness Zones, indicating the coldest region where a given plant can be reliably grown. The zones in North America are numbered north to south, which means the lower the number, the colder the climate. If you don't know the zone in the area where you live, ask at a local garden center or call the local master gardener hotline.

Zones	Species
4-9	arborescens, paniculata, petiolaris
5-9	quercifolia
6-9	macrophylla

IDEAL CONDITIONS

Whenever possible, choose plants for which you can provide ideal conditions. This makes it easier for both you and the plants to achieve satisfactory results. Don't despair, though, if you have less-than-ideal conditions. A determined gardener can learn to offset some of the problems inherent in the home garden. Poor soil can be amended. Winter protection can be provided for tender plants. Drainage can be improved. The important thing is to be aware of what constitutes ideal conditions for the plants you want to grow and to try to replicate those conditions as closely as possible.

Macrophylla (Mopheads & Lacecaps) Mopheads and lacecaps prefer morning sun and afternoon shade. The shrubs can thrive in full sun, but the flower heads will likely become browned and crisped eventually, either entirely or around the edges. You should aim for a rich, moist soil, with good drainage. An acidic soil is needed to produce blue flowers while a neutral or alkaline soil will produce pink flowers. As they are sensitive to temperature extremes, mopheads and lacecaps are happiest in a temperate climate and they really flourish in a moisture-rich coastal setting.

Paniculata (Panicle hydrangea) The paniculata thrives in full sun. It is adaptable so it can be grown in partial shade, particularly in the South, but if spectacular blooms are what you want, try to plant it in full sun. A sheltered site is best since these plants with their brittle stems are sensitive to wind. What constitutes a sheltered site? It is a location where the plant is protected from the full force of the wind. This doesn't mean the wind has to be completely blocked, as with a brick wall; something like a latticed fence would work perfectly well for this purpose.

Arborescens (Smooth-leafed hydrangea) The smooth-leafed hydrangea does well with consistent moisture, light shade, and a rich, acidic soil.

Quercifolia (Oakleaf hydrangea) This species is adaptable to either sun or shade as long as sufficient moisture is provided. As a native of the Southeastern United States, the oakleaf hydrangea seems to flower best with summer heat. It is able to flower in dense shade. A sheltered site is best as it is sensitive to wind.

Petiolaris (Climbing hydrangea) Climbing hydrangeas prefer partial shade. They are not too particular about soil, often thriving in poor soil, as long as the soil has good drainage.

Other Hydrangea Species The hydrangea species described in this chapter can keep you busy for quite a while, indeed, for a lifetime, but it is important to note there are many other hydrangea species worthy of consideration including *H. serrata, H. aspera, H. heteromala,* and *H. scandens.* You may find, as the author did, that interest in one species leads to another until the strong feeling develops that you want to know about all of them, but *where* are you going to find space for them in the garden? It becomes a very pleasant dilemma.

HOW TO SELECT HYDRANGEAS BY CLIMATE

3

*Choosing Plants Likely
to Thrive Where You Live*

The easiest way to succeed as a gardener is to use plant materials known to thrive in your area, to site them in the best possible locations in your garden, and to care for them appropriately. Since you are reading this book you must be interested in gracing your garden with at least one hydrangea. Before rushing out to buy a plant or plants you need to know whether your prevailing climate conditions are suitable for hydrangeas. If you look around and see lots of hydrangeas flourishing in nearby yards, you are in luck; your preliminary search is finished. But what if you haven't seen any hydrangeas in your area? How can you find out if hydrangeas will thrive in your own yard?

Everyone, consciously or unconsciously, knows what constitutes their own perfect weather conditions; so too with plants. Some need heat to thrive. Some need the long dormant period provided by cold winters. Some are happy in the sun while others long for the shade. Knowing what your plants need and making sure their needs are satisfied are keys to success in gardening. Local garden centers usually stock plants known to do well in your area. But what if you see a plant you like in a magazine or garden catalog and it says "zones 6-9". What does that mean?

Hardiness Zones

In the 1930s the United States Department of Agriculture came up with a hardiness zone map, which has been periodically updated. It is a system designed to let growers know which plants are likely to survive winter in their part of the country. The country is divided into eleven temperature zones based on the average annual low temperature. The country is divided from north to south, i.e. from the coldest climates to the warmest. The range in winter low temperatures goes from -50 degrees in Zone 1 to 40 degrees in Zone 11.

If a plant description indicates "Zones 6-9", it means that plant is winter hardy down to ten degrees below zero (Zone 6). A range of 6-9 and not 6-11 indicates the plants need some cold temperatures in the winter to go into a period of dormancy. Most mophead and lacecap hydrangeas (the macrophyllas) are in zones 6-9 (a few are considered cold hardy down to zone 5). The climate in Georgia (the home of the American Hydrangea Society) ranges from zones 6-8; it is no surprise that hydrangeas flourish there!

Zone	Average Annual Minimum Temperature
1	-50 degrees or below
2	-50 degrees to -40 degrees
3	-40 degrees to -30 degrees
4	-30 degrees to -20 degrees
5	-20 degrees to -10 degrees
6	-10 degrees to zero degrees
7	zero degrees to 10 degrees
8	10 degrees to 20 degrees
9	20 degrees to 30 degrees
10	30 degrees to 40 degrees
11	40 degrees and above

It is common to find more than one zone represented within a given state; in some cases the winter temperature range is quite extensive. You might expect Alaska to fall into the coldest ranges exclusively and, indeed, the bulk of the state is divided into zones 1-4, but there are small pockets, particularly in or around the Gulf of Alaska that fall within zones 5-7.

The author lived in Portland, Oregon, for fourteen years and found its zone 8 climate wonderful for gardening. Portland's location between the coast and the Cascade mountain range provided a moderate climate. East of the mountains the climate is vastly different; it is much colder in the winter. The mountain range serves to block the moderating effect of the warmer air from the coast. This is a state with vastly different microclimates, from the fertile Willamette Valley to the high desert country east of the Cascades.

In Massachusetts climate zones range from zone 5 in the western part of the state which includes the Berkshire Mountains to zone 7 on Cape Cod with its maritime influence, while most of the eastern part of the state is in zone 6. Hydrangeas flourish on Cape Cod, with only the most tender varieties needing winter

Hydrangeas flourish in Cape Cod's maritime climate.

A foggy day in Chatham, Massachusetts. The extra moisture provided by fog helps hydrangeas thrive here.

Healthy lush hydrangeas are the norm on Cape Cod.

protection. Gardeners in western Massachusetts, however, need to provide winter protection if they want their plants to produce flowers.

Please note, the various species of hydrangeas react differently to cold temperatures and thus the range of hardiness zones varies as well. When you look at the breakdown below, you will understand why gardeners in Minnesota (zone 4) have had little luck with mopheads and lacecaps (macrophyllas); the average winter low temperatures are just too cold for them. Until recently a Minnesota gardener longing for blue mopheads would either have to provide winter protection or be resigned to winter kill.

Zones	Species
4-9	arborescens, paniculata, petiolaris
5-9	quercifolia
6-9	macrophylla

Recent discoveries and systematic breeding programs have offered hope to gardeners living in climates colder than the normal range for mopheads and lacecaps. Endless Summer® and other remontant varieties ('David Ramsey', 'Decatur Blue', 'Oak Hill', 'Penny Mac', and Endless Summer® 'Blushing Bride') bloom on new wood. Previously all macrophyllas bloomed on old wood,

meaning stems that grew and set bud in the previous growing season. "Remontant" means flowering more than once in a single season. If the buds on a remontant variety fail to survive the winter or a freeze after a spring thaw, the plant will set new buds on the new season's growth and flowers will appear that same year. These new, remontant hydrangea macrophylla varieties are different from most macrophyllas. Most mopheads and lacecaps set their buds on old wood (the previous year's growth) and if the buds are killed off, that's that. No chance for flowers at all for a whole growing season. This is, of course, very discouraging for any gardener looking forward to many weeks of beautiful flowers during the summer. The remontant varieties mentioned above are all mopheads. A newly introduced remontant lacecap is called Twist-n-Shout®.

Microclimates

Naturally you need to determine the hardiness zone for your growing area. You also should know that individual gardens can have many microclimates, such that conditions can be significantly different from one part of the yard to another. Some areas are sunnier than others. Some are subjected to buffeting winds. Planting close to the foundation of the house can provide extra warmth and wind protection for tender plants. Low lying areas can encourage pooling of rainwater; plants that need good drainage (like hydrangeas) would not do well here. Pay attention to the sunlight particularly. You will want to know how much sun each area gets and at what time of the day. Morning light is less harsh than afternoon sun.

This lawn at Wychmere Harbor in Harwich is a frequent site of summer weddings where the natural beauty of the ocean and a lush row of hydrangeas accent the special day for the bride and groom.

Lacecaps thriving in the sea air on the island of Nantucket. These shrubs with abundant blooms are just steps away from the water of Nantucket Harbor.

Hydrangeas near the Harwich shoreline on Cape Cod.

Maritime Climate

If you live in a maritime climate you are lucky, indeed, when it comes to growing hydrangeas. As most hydrangeas originated in this kind of climate, they are happy and likely to thrive in seaside communities where they feel at home.

How to determine your hardiness zone

The easiest way to discover your region's hardiness zone is to ask at a local garden center. Or check this handy website: http://www.garden.org/zipzone/ provided by the National Gardening Association. You simply plug in your zip code and the search engine reveals your hardiness zone. Another strategy is to check the gardening section at your local library or ask the research librarian to help you find the information. Members of local gardening clubs are also likely to know the hardiness zone for your area.

Mopheads on Straight Wharf in Nantucket are among the first visual pleasures enjoyed by day trippers as they leave the ferry from Cape Cod.

A short stroll along Water Street in Edgartown on the island of Martha's Vineyard makes clear how popular hydrangeas are here and how magnificently they thrive in the sea air.

Lush hydrangeas surround the Korean War Memorial in Hyannis's Veterans Park.

HOW TO SELECT HYDRANGEAS BY SIZE

4

Anticipating Growth

Finding the right size hydrangea for that particular spot in your garden requires some thought. Too often we fall in love with a beautiful plant at the garden center and plunk it down in the garden where we think it will be perfect without considering its eventual size. It is unfortunate when we become dismayed by a plant that once pleased us. The plant we once loved is now considered a thug in the garden because it has overgrown its space. It has either grown too tall, too wide, or both. Good planning will help you avoid that problem.

Fortunately there are hydrangeas to suit every size requirement, from compact two-foot mopheads to paniculatas that soar up to fifteen feet or more. Plant labels at garden centers often reveal this information, but not every plant is well labeled. For this reason it is a good idea to have in mind the typical mature size so that you know, before leaving your house, whether that species is apt to be a good choice for that spot.

This chapter details the typical size range for each species. The eventual height of the plant is one vital piece of information with the other being its normal

Hydrangea paniculata 'Unique', planted where it has room to grow even taller than its current eight feet. A plant in the right conditions can easily exceed the normal height range suggested on plant labels.

spread. With these details you can make some good Goldilocks-type assessments about whether the plant will eventually be too large, too small, or just right.

Also noted are particular varieties at both the small end and the large end of the scale. Whether your garden is a tiny courtyard or an expansive estate you should be able to find the right size hydrangeas to work within the space and look appropriate.

Typical Size Range of Macrophyllas

Mopheads. Most mopheads grow to be about five feet tall and just as wide. It is hard to remember this when you see the cute little knee-high plant in its container at the garden center. Too often mopheads are planted where they block the views from windows or create a navigation problem getting to a door. These situations lead to a great

A good label at a garden center will predict the plant's ultimate mature size. This 'Nikko Blue' will probably be four to six feet high and equally wide.

These mopheads have plenty of room to grow taller and wider.

The mopheads in these raised beds are situated perfectly. They can grow taller and wider without blocking easy access to the front door of the house.

The height of this mophead hydrangea is not a problem, but the plant has grown outward as well as upward, a factor that is commonly overlooked. Now this homeowner will have to fight the plant to provide easy access to the door. As often as it is pruned back it will grow back, aiming to be the height and width it wants to be.

deal of frustration and misguided attempts to keep the plants to the desired size with constant pruning. Constant pruning often leads to a lack of flowers, compounding the problem. The mophead in this kind of situation will keep fighting you because it wants to be the size it was intended to be: five feet tall and five feet wide. It is better to plant a smaller variety in the first place so you don't have this struggle down the line.

Mopheads three feet and under: the Cityline™ series including Berlin, Mars, Paris, Rio, Venice, and Vienna (the smallest of the series); the Halo Hydrangeas™ series (all bicolor) including Angel Eyes™ and Angel Smile™; 'Harlequin'; 'Hörnli'; 'Pia' (also known as Pink Elf®); Sabrina™; and Stella™.

Mopheads three to four feet tall: 'All Summer Beauty'; 'Alpenglühen'; 'Amethyst'; 'Ami Pasquier'; 'Blauer Zwerg'; 'Blue Danube'; 'Böttstein'; 'Bouquet Rose'; 'Brunette'; 'Forever Pink'; 'Masja'; 'Merritt's Supreme'; Mini Penny™; 'Miss Belgium'; 'Purple Majesty'; 'Red Star'; 'Regula'; "Tödi'; 'Tovelit'; and 'Trophée'.

It is a good idea to seek out smaller plants when space is limited. 'Compacta', the flower-filled shrub in the foreground, is a good selection for small areas.

Hydrangeas of varying mature sizes were chosen for this garden bed. The dwarf varieties under the window will always be small enough so that the window will not be blocked.

29

Tall mopheads: 'Big Daddy'; 'Générale Vicomtesse de Vibraye'; 'Goliath'; 'King George'; 'Niedersachsen'; 'Penny Mac'; and 'Souvenir du Pdt. Paul Doumer'.

Lacecaps. Lacecaps usually attain a mature size of five feet or more. Smaller varieties are noted below.

Lacecap three feet and under: Angel Lace™.

Lacecaps three to four feet tall: 'Izu-no-Hana'; 'Shamrock'; 'Sol'; and 'Zaunkönig'.

Good luck trying to see anything except this lacecap hydrangea from inside.

A lacecap with plenty of room to grow larger.

Typical Size Range of Paniculatas

Paniculatas can be grown as large shrubs or small trees. Many of the cultivars range from six to

Fairly young hydrangeas will clearly grow higher and wider. The paniculata in the center can easily be kept in check with pruning at any time of the year. The mopheads, however, may impinge upon the sidewalk as they grow both taller and wider.

This beautiful display of paniculatas at the Chatham Bars Inn has been well sited. The individual plants were located far enough back from the brick path to allow free pedestrian traffic. The author at 5'4" will never achieve the height of these plants. *Photo by Susan Dalton.*

eight feet tall. Both shorter and taller cultivars are noted below.

Petite paniculatas: 'Bombshell'; 'Dharuma'; 'Kyushu'; Little Lime™; 'Pee Wee'; and White Diamonds™.

Tall paniculatas: 'Burgundy Lace' (10-14'); 'Grandiflora' (8-10'); 'Mount Everest' (12'+); and 'Unique' (10-14').

Typical Size Range of Oakleaf Hydrangeas

Oakleaf hydrangeas tend to range from four to six feet.

Small oakleaf varieties: 'Little Honey'; 'Pee Wee'; 'Ruby Slippers'; 'Munchkin'; and 'Sikes Dwarf'.

Large oakleaf varieties: 'Alice'; 'Alison'; 'Snowflake'; and 'Snow Giant'.

Be prepared for an oakleaf hydrangea in good conditions to grow to an impressive size. This oakleaf is located in Atlanta, Georgia where the oakleafs thrive.

A white garden in Harwich, Massachusetts, with a sweep of *Hydrangea arborescens* 'Annabelle' on the left and a single oakleaf hydrangea on the right. All plants have plenty of room to grow.

Typical Size Range of Arborescens

Hydrangea arborescens varieties generally range from three to six feet tall. 'Hayes Starburst' is at the smaller end of that scale.

Exceptions to the rule

Keep in mind that some hydrangeas under certain conditions can violate the general guidelines outlined above. If the plant has ideal conditions it may be much taller and wider than the norm. A plant with adverse conditions could be smaller than the norm. What the grower is really saying is that this plant will *probably* be x tall and x wide. The guidelines are helpful because most hydrangeas will fall within the normal size range.

When the Amount of Space is More Than Sufficient

If you have chosen to plant a hydrangea variety all by itself, size is no longer an issue in the sense that you don't have to worry about its outgrowing its space. There's a lot to be said for so-called "specimen plants". The eye is drawn to them because of their isolation.

Hydrangea macrophylla 'Alpenglühen' adjacent to a sundial. 'Alpenglühen' was selected for this spot for its color and mature size which is unlikely ever to overwhelm the sundial.

Varying heights adds interest to the garden

Hydrangeas make excellent companions for each other because of the wide range of plant height at maturity. Whether you need a dwarf plant to fill a space under a window or a very tall plant to camouflage an unsightly view, you should be able to find a hydrangea to satisfy your needs.

Hydrangeas located in perfect conditions tend to grow very large. This mophead and lacecap are situated across the street from Hyannis Harbor on Cape Cod.

A mophead with plenty of room to grow.

Hydrangeas can be quite large near the entrance to a house if they are placed correctly.

HOW TO SELECT HYDRANGEAS BY SUN AND SHADE REQUIREMENTS

Providing Sunlight in the Right Amounts at the Right Time of Day

Plants need varying degrees of sunlight. As a gardener you know there are sun-loving plants and shade-loving plants and plants that tolerate mixed conditions. This chapter details the sun/shade requirements for the five species of hydrangeas covered in this book.

Geography plays a role in how much sun a plant can tolerate. A particular variety might tolerate full sun in a moist maritime climate but need more shade in a hot and dry climate where plants can dry out too quickly and flowers become scorched. When in doubt, try for morning sun and afternoon shade.

In addition to the guidelines presented here, be sure to check plant labels when purchasing the plant. Garden center personnel are usually trained to answer questions about sun requirements and the plants are often (but not always) placed in the best possible conditions at the point of sale.

Blue mopheads on Nantucket with good sun/shade conditions. This photo was taken at 3:30 in the afternoon. Afternoon shade like this helps to prevent scorching of flowers that can occur when the sun is too intense.

Macrophyllas (mopheads and lacecaps)

Ideally mopheads and lacecaps should be planted where they will get morning sun and afternoon shade. Some varieties can tolerate full sun, especially in a maritime climate, but the flower color will fade faster than if they had protection from the intense afternoon sun. There is also a danger of the flowers becoming scorched. You don't want to place them where they get too much shade though. This species needs several hours of daily sunshine for good flowering. A frequent cause of lack of flowers is too much shade.

Hydrangeas and roses in full sun throughout the day. This photo was taken in early July when the blue mopheads still look good. Because they are not protected from afternoon sun, the flower color will fade and some of the flowers will become scorched.

The tree branches provide shade in the afternoon when the sun is most intense. Because the hydrangeas receive ideal conditions, morning sun and afternoon shade, the flower colors are strong and long-lasting.

Despite being planted under a tree these hydrangeas get several hours of morning sun.

By late August on Cape Cod, when this photo was taken, mophead flowers in full sun often show signs of scorching. If this same plant had protection from the afternoon sun, all the flowers would still look unblemished, with rich full color.

Look for dark glossy leaves on mopheads or lacecaps if you want plants that are more likely to resist sun and wind damage. Notice the leaves of 'Masja' are clearly darker and more glossy than the two other varieties.

Sun tolerant mopheads: 'Alpenglühen'(a.k.a. 'Glowing Embers'); 'Altona'; 'Ami Pasquier'; 'Ayesha'; 'Blauer Prinz'; 'Böttstein'; 'Enziandom'; 'Forever Pink'; 'Masja'; and 'Otaksa'.

Hydrangea macrophylla 'Masja', a magnificent plant in full sun.

Sun tolerant lacecaps: 'Blue Wave'; 'Geoffrey Chadbund'; 'Lanarth White'; 'Lilacina'; and 'Tokyo Delight'.

A clue to sun tolerance in macrophyllas: look at the foliage. Mopheads and lacecaps with dark shiny leaves usually tolerate the sun more than those with matte leaves. There is a trade-off, however. Macrophyllas with shiny leaves tend to break bud early which makes them susceptible to damage from late frosts. The climate zone range recommended for macrophyllas extends from Zone 6 (the coldest) to Zone 9 (the warmest). If you live in Zone 6 you might want to look for mopheads and lacecap varieties with matte leaves instead of the shiny leaves, as they will do better at resisting the cold.

Paniculatas

The paniculata thrives in full sun. It is adaptable to conditions so it can be grown in partial shade, particularly in the South, but if spectacular blooms are what you want, try to plant it in full sun.

Quercifolias (oakleafs)

This species is native to the southeastern United States where it is happy in all sunlight conditions from full sun to full shade.

Paniculatas enjoy full sun at the Chatham Bars Inn on Cape Cod.

Arborescens

Another native of the southeastern United States, this species will do well in full sun, partial sun, and shade.

Hydrangea arborescens 'Annabelle' is flexible as to sun/shade conditions. Here it is in full sun in the foreground while it also adds brightness to the shady conditions in the background.

Several plantings of *Hydrangea arborescens* 'Annabelle' provide a strong backdrop to this lovely shade garden on Cape Cod.

Climbing hydrangea

This species does well in partial shade but can tolerate full sun, especially in northern climates.

Importance of water

The amount of sun hydrangeas can tolerate depends on the species but the availability of water is also an important consideration. If your hydrangeas are kept well watered they can tolerate more sun than they would if subjected to the stress of insufficient moisture. Mulching around your plants will help the soil retain moisture.

At the Wayside Inn in Chatham, Massachusetts, the hydrangeas have been sited appropriately according to sun conditions. The white flowers of *Hydrangea arborescens* 'Annabelle' do well in full sun, while the blue mopheads in the background are happier in afternoon shade.

HOW TO ACHIEVE THE DESIRED COLOR

6

Clearing Up Color Mysteries

There is a great deal of confusion about the characteristic color of particular hydrangea varieties, since they are unique in their ability to change color depending on the pH of the soil. It is not unusual to see rows of 'Nikko Blue' hydrangeas at a garden center all sporting pink flowers. Similarly, 'Forever Pink' can be covered in blue flowers. Sometimes when a plant is moved from one part of the garden to another, the flowers temporarily change color. Baby plants grown from cuttings taken from a blue hydrangea often first flower in shades of pink. No wonder people get confused!

If you have no color preference for your hydrangeas feel free to skip this section. For those of you who do have a preference, the explanations below are designed to give you a fighting chance to get the color you want. You need to know that sometimes the color you want comes naturally, sometimes you have to work to achieve the desired color, and sometimes the shrub in your garden is not going to produce the color flowers you want no matter what you do. Let's address each of these in turn.

Blue mopheads are prevalent in areas where the soil tends to be acidic. Many of Cape Cod's hydrangeas appear in various shades of blue.

Pink mopheads are more common in areas where the soil tends to be alkaline. This photo was taken in England where the pinks are prevalent.

Colors Produced Naturally

Two conditions satisfied will naturally produce the flower colors you desire. First, select a hydrangea variety known for flowers in that particular color. Second, have soil favorable to producing that color.

Let's say the starting point is a desire for blue hydrangea flowers. Before you buy the plant you also need to think about the soil in your garden. You don't need to know anything about soil pH at this point; just look around the area where you live. If most hydrangea shrubs in your part of the world produce blue flowers you probably have an acidic soil; if pink, you probably have an alkaline soil. This is not a guarantee, but it is a reasonable guide.

Blue flowers are common in the Pacific Northwest where frequent rainfall tends to make the soil acidic. If you tour Cape Cod, Massachusetts, in the summertime you will see blue hydrangeas everywhere. Faial, an island in the Azores, is often called the "blue island" because of the blue hydrangeas that form tall hedges all over the island. It is not impossible to achieve pink flowers in these places but the gardener seeking to do so would be swimming against the tide. Other parts of the world where the soil is more alkaline routinely produce pink flowers. They are easy to find in sections of California as well as in England and Ireland. Lucky are the gardeners who love the prevailing color in their area.

If you want blue hydrangea flowers and you live where blue hydrangea flowers are common you will likely get some shade of blue without any extra effort on your part. Similarly, if you want pink hydrangea flowers and you live where pink hydrangea flowers are common you will likely get some shade of pink without extra effort. Notice these statements are qualified with the word "likely". Some varieties are

H.m. 'Générale Vicomtesse de Vibraye' produces pale blue flowers in an acidic soil.

A Nantucket homeowner loves this hydrangea shrub which produces mopheads in a medium shade of blue.

A deep blue mophead is set off nicely in a pale green basket.

known to resist color changes. Most varieties, however, will follow this pattern. Also notice the words **"some shade of blue"** and **"some shade of pink"**. Blues can be pale blue, medium blue, or deep blue. Pinks can also range from pale shades to deep shades. To get the shade you want you have to select the right variety. Many suggestions are provided later in this chapter. Finally please note that soil pH doesn't affect white hydrangeas. You cannot expect a white hydrangea to become blue or pink; it will remain white.

To summarize: **The right hydrangea variety + the right soil = the desired color.** The right hydrangea variety is one that is known to produce the color you seek. If you want a deep blue flower you need to plant a variety known to produce deep blue

Hydrangea macrophylla 'Bits of Lace' produces pale pink flowers.

A medium pink mophead spotted in Anderson, South Carolina.

H.m. Cityline™ 'Paris' produces flowers in a rich deep pink shade.

flowers in acidic soil. The right soil depends on the color you want. If you want blue flowers the right soil is acidic. If you want pink flowers the right soil is alkaline. What if you want to grow a mix of colors in your garden? The rule still applies because, in this case, the right soil is slightly acidic which can support a wide range of colors.

Working to Achieve the Desired Color

So what is all this about the soil's pH? It just refers to the relative acidity of the soil. Soil that is balanced between the extremes of acid or alkaline is said to be neutral. Soils with low pH are acidic and those with high pH are alkaline. If you see blue hydrangeas all around where you live, you probably have an acidic soil in your garden. If you see pink hydrangeas all around you, your garden soil is probably alkaline. Lacking those obvious clues you can use a soil test kit to find out the pH of your garden soil, or send a sample to your local university extension service. A master gardener hotline is a good resource to find out how and where to get your soil tested.

Most garden soils contain aluminum and it is that which leads to blue flowers; acidic soils allow the aluminum to be absorbed by the plant while alkaline soils bind up the aluminum, blocking its

absorption. The home gardener can counteract the natural process by amending the soil. To get blue flowers in an alkaline soil, add aluminum sulfate. To get pink flowers in acidic soil, add lime.

Aluminum sulfate and lime are available at garden centers. Dolomite lime is best. Make sure you follow the package directions. For aluminum sulfate it may say something like this: *Add 1 tablespoon to 1 gallon of water and soak around the drip line of the plant.* The amount of dolomite lime will depend on the size of the plant. A small plant might require ¼ cup while a large plant might require 3 cups. Follow the package directions for correct amounts, apply it uniformly around the drip line of the plant and water it in well. It is a good idea to read the package directions before buying the product. If you are at all unsure, it is best to check with garden center personnel before you head home.

The best time to apply amendments is in the spring when the flower buds first appear. A good rule of thumb is to space three or four treatments at two-week intervals (treatment #1, wait two weeks, treatment #2, wait two weeks, etc.). At each treatment make sure you water it in well because you want to encourage the product to get down to the roots.

Caution: Aluminum sulfate can be toxic to plants. Don't make the mistake of thinking more is better; you could kill the plant.

Color Won't Change No Matter What You Do

You can work to change hydrangea flower color from **blue to pink** or from **pink to blue,** but there's nothing you can do to change a white hydrangea flower to either of these colors. White hydrangeas are not subject to the same pH influences. Whites tend to stay white until the end of the growing season when they might go through various color changes as they age but this has nothing to do with soil pH.

Note: You can change the color of a hydrangea flower from blue to pink but the **intensity** of color tends to remain the same. A light blue flower becomes a light pink flower; medium blue becomes medium pink; and deep blue becomes deep pink (and vice versa in each case, depending on the soil). If your hydrangea sports pale blue flowers and you really want deep cobalt blue flowers you need to buy another shrub, one known to produce deep blue flowers. The best you can do with the pale blue flowers is to help them look their best; an attractive pale blue, not a washed out shade. Siting the plant well (morning sun and afternoon shade) and providing appropriate fertilizer to keep the plant healthy will help produce the best color possible.

H.m. 'Madame Emile Mouillère' is a white mophead with an interesting characteristic. Its "eyes" are blue in acidic soils and pink in alkaline soils. How often can you look into a flower's eyes to learn something about the pH of the soil?

H.m. 'Blushing Bride' is a beautiful white mophead in the Endless Summer™ collection.

A few hydrangea varieties are known to resist color changes and this trait is usually noted in the plant description. *Hydrangea*

White mopheads frequently take on a speckled appearance late in the season. This 'Blushing Bride' was pure white for many weeks before taking on a variety of colors in mid-October on Cape Cod.

macrophylla 'Alpengluhen', for instance, wants to produce pink flowers even in acidic soil. This is not a guarantee. It is just that it is more likely to resist the color changes than some other varieties.

Blue Hydrangea Flowers

As noted above if the hydrangeas in the part of the world where you live tend to be blue the chances are good that yours will be too. Now it is just a matter of selecting the intensity of blue you prefer: pale blue, medium blue, or deep blue.

The descriptive words for blue hydrangeas used in catalogues and garden centers may be helpful or confusing depending on what

Some hydrangeas resist color changes. H.m. 'Alpenglühen' (a.k.a. 'Glowing Embers'), shown here, often remains pink in acidic soil, even while the flowers of other hydrangeas in the same garden have become blue.

Hydrangeas known to resist color changes don't always resist the changes. This 'Alpenglühen' flower has turned blue in the acidic soil of the Cape Cod Hydrangea Society's display garden at Heritage Gardens, but notice the edges have remained pink.

associations you have with these words. The following are only some of the many descriptions the author has encountered: Persian blue, bluebird blue, dark blue, gentian blue, soft blue, sky blue, pale blue, royal blue, rich blue, Wedgwood blue, flax blue, light blue, powder blue, cobalt blue, French blue, and cornflower blue.

The multiplicity of terms is further complicated by subjectivity; the quality of blue is in the eye of the beholder. Your cornflower blue might be another person's royal blue. The table below will provide a starting point but expect some trial and error before you find the ideal shade of blue for you. (**Note:** for **blue** hydrangeas look for a **fertilizer** with an NPK ratio of 25/5/30.)

Light Blue	Medium Blue	Dark Blue
'Domotoi'	'Dooley'	'Altona'
'Frillibet'	'Nikko Blue'	'Blue Danube'
'La Marne'	'Penny Mac'	'Hamburg'
'Otaksa'	'La France'	'Enziandom' (a.k.a. 'Gentian Dome')
'Mousseline'	'Gartenbau-direktor Kühnert'	
'Niedersachsen'	'Mme Faustin Travouillon'	
'Générale Vicomtesse de Vibraye'	Endless Summer®	

All of the hydrangea varieties in the table are mopheads. For a pale blue lacecap try 'Lanarth Lavender'. 'Lilacina' is a medium blue lacecap. Two excellent deep blue lacecaps are 'Blaumeise' and 'Taube'.

Note: If flower color is important to you and you are selecting from a catalogue, don't base your decision solely on the picture provided; make sure you read the description. The author has seen pictures of hydrangeas

with light blue flowers described as "deep cobalt blue". The description is more likely to be accurate than the picture but still it is wise to check with the source whenever you encounter this kind of contradiction.

Pink Hydrangea Flowers

As with blue hydrangeas, pink hydrangea flowers are available in many shades and these are described using language that may or may not resonate with you. Some of the descriptive words used are soft pink, pale pink, mauve, blushing pink, pretty pink, deep pink, vivid pink, bright pink, cherry pink, salmon pink, phlox pink, rosy pink, hot pink, rich Persian rose, rose-madder, crimson-pink, rich pink, neon pink, medium pink, pastel pink, dusty pink, pink cotton candy, and delicate pink. You could make a good guess about the ultimate color using these words as guidelines, but it is still a guess. What, for instance, would differentiate a "vivid pink" flower from a "bright pink" flower? Is one darker than the other? Or is your vivid pink my bright pink? The table for hydrangeas with pink flowers should help somewhat, at least by grouping the flowers by intensity of color (light, medium and dark) but expect some trial and error before you find what you would label *perfect* pink. (**Note:** for **pink** hydrangeas look for a **fertilizer** with an NPK ratio of 25/10/10.)

Light Pink	Medium Pink	Dark Pink
'Amethyst'	'All Summer Beauty'	'Alpenglühen'
'Blushing Pink'	'Big Daddy'	'Europa'
'Bouquet Rose'	'Brestenberg'	'Haworth Booth'
'Domotoi'	'Dooley'	'Kasteln'
'Frillibet'	'Forever Pink'	'Masja'
'La Marne'	'King George'	'Merritt's Supreme'
'Mousseline'	'Penny Mac'	'Red Star'

Some varieties, you may have noticed, appear on both lists, blue and pink. The reason goes back to the pH of the soil which affects the color of many hydrangea varieties. 'Domotoi' is light blue in acidic soil and light pink in alkaline soil. The color may change but the intensity of color is not likely to change; a light blue changes to light pink but not deep pink. A deep blue changes to deep pink not light pink.

The table for hydrangeas with pink flowers lists mopheads exclusively. If you want a light pink lacecap try 'Hobella'. For a medium pink, try 'Mousmé'. Two deep pink lacecaps are 'Geoffrey Chadbund' and 'Kardinal'.

Red Hydrangea Flowers

There is some disagreement as to whether some hydrangea flowers are really red or rather a very deep pink. The perception of color is influenced by neighboring colors in the garden. A deep pink hydrangea flower can look red if it is located next to a light pink flower. But the same deep pink hydrangea can look pink next to a red geranium. If you are looking for hydrangea flowers that are true red you may be disappointed. If, on the other hand, you would be happy with "reddish", you might want to give one or more of the following varieties a try.

Mopheads with reddish flowers: 'Alpenglühen', 'Böttstein', 'Cardinal Red', 'Haworth Booth', 'Hörnli', 'Masja', 'Merritt's Beauty', 'Oregon Pride', 'Red Star', 'Révélation', and 'Westfalen'. Lacecaps with reddish flowers: 'Blaumeise', 'Fasan', 'Geoffrey Chadbund', 'Kardinal', 'Nightingale', 'Rotdrossel' ('Teller Red'), and 'Rotschwantz' ('Red Start').

Purple Hydrangea Flowers

Purple hydrangea flowers range from shades of soft lavender to deep purple. The colors are variously described as pale violet, lavender, lilac, wine purple, violet blue, purplish blue, purple, dark lavender, pinkish purple, rich blue-purple, deep purple, and inky purple. Purple hydrangeas tend to be deep purple. The following list provides options in the purple family.

Soft lavender mopheads: 'Amethyst' and 'Ayesha'.

Medium purple mopheads: 'Heinrich Seidel' and 'Königin Wilhelmina'.

Medium purple lacecap: 'Fasan'.

Deep purple mopheads: 'Ami Pasquier', 'Brunette', 'Europa', 'Flamboyant', 'Freudenstein', 'Gertrude Glahn', 'Holehird Purple', 'Hörnli', 'Kluis Superba', 'Lady Fujiyo', 'Leuchtfeuer', 'Masja', 'Mathilda Gutges', 'Merritt's Supreme', 'Miss Belgium', 'Miss Hepburn', 'Oregon Pride', 'Paris', 'Princess Beatrix', 'Purple Majesty', 'Souvenir du Président Paul Doumer', and 'Violetta'.

H.m. 'Ayesha' with lavender flowers.

The flowers of H.m. 'Sister Theresa' light up a section of the Atlanta Botanical Garden.

White Mophead and Lacecap Flowers

White hydrangeas do not make drastic color changes depending on the pH of the soil, as do the blues and the pinks. You cannot change a flower color from white to blue or white to pink. White hydrangeas can change color but these color changes are usually the result of seasonal changes not soil composition.

Mopheads with white flowers: Endless Summer® 'Blushing Bride', 'Le Cygne', 'Madame Emile Mouillère', 'Patio White', 'Queen of Pearls', 'Regula', 'Sister Theresa', and 'Princess Juliana'.

The white lacecap, 'Tokyo Delight', flowers abundantly.

Deep purple lacecaps: 'Eisvogel' (a.k.a. 'Teller Purple'), 'Geoffrey Chadbund', 'Möwe', 'Nightingale', 'Kardinal', 'Mousmé', 'Rotdrossel', and 'Zaunkönig'.

Note: Remember that the pH of your soil influences the flower color. If your flowers are more blue than purple you might want to amend the soil with a little lime. If the flowers are more pink than purple, add aluminum sulfate. The ideal soil for purples seems to be right in the middle of the pH scale; neither acidic nor alkaline.

The large white "snowball" flowers of H.a.'Annabelle' in a Harwich, Massachusetts, garden.

The large flowers of oakleaf hydrangeas are pure white during most of the growing season before they change to shades of pink and ultimately to chocolate brown.

Lacecaps with white flowers: 'Beauté Vendômoise', 'Lanarth White', 'Libelle', 'Tokyo Delight', 'Veitchii', 'Wayne's White', and 'White Wave'.

White Flowers on Other Hydrangea Species

The flowers of most paniculata, arborescens, and oakleaf hydrangeas are white in their prime blooming season. Many white hydrangeas change color as the seasons progress. The flowers on *Hydrangea arborescens* 'Annabelle' are green when they first emerge in the spring, white all summer, and green again in the fall. Many of the paniculatas change from white to ever deepening shades of pink to burgundy. Some oakleaf hydrangea flowers change from white to pink to chocolate brown.

As any decorator will tell you, there are countless shades of white. The terms used to describe white hydrangea flowers include pure white, creamy white, ivory, wedding white, pearly white, snow white, and paper white.

White flowers look wonderful when massed together and are natural companion plants for a wide variety of other plants. Fortunately for the home gardener it is easy to find white hydrangea flowers with bloom times from early spring (climbing hydrangeas and lacecaps) through summer (mopheads, oakleafs, arborescens) and well into the fall (paniculatas).

This photo was taken early in the growing season on Cape Cod when it is not unusual to see mopheads sporting many colors simultaneously. Eventually all these flowers turned a medium shade of blue.

Green Hydrangea Flowers

Most green hydrangea flowers were a different color earlier and then aged to a shade of green. The lacecap 'White Wave', for instance, tends to age to light green. 'Dooley' is a medium blue mophead that ages to a medium green. H.m. 'Queen of Pearls' starts off with green flowers that turn pure white and then age back to green. Other mopheads that tend to age to green are 'Renate Steiniger', 'Berlin', and 'Stene's Pink'. Big, round green flower heads spotted in the spring are either immature mopheads that haven't had time to develop their color yet, or a variety of *Hydrangea arborescens*. H.a. 'Annabelle' flowers are green when

This flower appeared in the middle of the summer on a shrub where all the other flowers were solid blue. It, too, eventually turned solid blue.

H.m. 'Harlequin' in a Yarmouth Port, Massachusetts, garden.

H.m. Angel Wings™ at Mal Condon's Hydrangea Farm on Nantucket.

they first emerge, turn pure white during the summer and fade back to green in the fall. 'Green Knight' is another arborescens variety with flowers that age to green. The *Hydrangea paniculata* 'Limelight' also starts out green before it turns white and then pink in the fall and possibly back to green again.

Multicolored Flowers

Sometimes many colors appear on the same flower. It is not unusual for this to happen to the flowers all over a shrub in the early spring when the colors are still in the process of developing. Eventually the flowers settle on the one color they will show for the bulk of the growing season. A multicolored flower is most striking when it is the only one on the plant. Somehow the feeder roots for this individual flower are

not absorbing sufficient aluminum to make the flower all blue. The parts of the flower that are getting sufficient aluminum are blue; parts that are getting less aluminum may be lavender, and parts getting no aluminum are pink; hence the

H.m. 'Ravel' at Mal Condon's Hydrangea Farm.

multicolored effect. Two hydrangea varieties that have a tendency to produce flowers of many colors at the same time are 'Mathilda Gutges' and 'Parzifal'.

Some gardeners enjoy playing with soil amendments to try to

Twist-n-Shout
With a botanic name like *Hydrangea macrophylla* 'PIIHM' it's no wonder that most prefer to use the common name for this shrub: Twist-n-Shout!

This lacecap is in the Endless Summer Collection so you can be sure it will bloom on both new and old growth.

Lacy pink or blue flowers ~end~ and dark, glossy le ~ed stems~ Shout will grow b ~Twist-n-~ morning sun and ~nt in~ compost or com ~ll with~

Prune Twist-n ~ unsightly gr~

H.m. Twist-n-Shout® can produce pink flowers in an alkaline or neutral soil or blue flowers in an acidic soil.

achieve the same multicolored effects produced naturally by Mother Nature. Should you want to try this, you will improve the likelihood of success if you plant the hydrangea in a container with good quality potting soil. Add appropriate amounts of aluminum sulfate to the soil on two opposite sides of the container and appropriate amounts of dolomite lime to the soil on the remaining opposite sides. ("Appropriate" amounts are based on package directions.) Remember, soil amendments can be toxic if they exceed the recommended amounts.

A few hydrangea varieties have a two-toned effect called picotee, a term applied when the edge contrasts with the flower's base color. The flower might be a blue, pink, or purple hydrangea edged in white such as 'Harlequin', or white with a contrasting edge in a darker color, such as Sabrina™ in the Dutch Lady series. These hydrangeas tend to be more tender (i.e. less frost hardy) than others, so appropriate care should be taken. Many gardeners in colder climates choose to grow these varieties in pots and overwinter them in an unheated basement where the temperature is not apt to dip below freezing.

Plant breeders have introduced several new hydrangea varieties with picotee edges in recent years adding to the previous standby, 'Harlequin'. These include the Halo™ series and some of the varieties in the Dutch Lady™ series.

Flower Color Changes in Autumn

Most hydrangea flowers change color noticeably as they mature. A flower that is bright blue in summer may be a deep burgundy in the fall. Many hydrangeas turn green as they age. Some flowers become quite spotted. Recognize that it is normal for these changes to occur. The colors you loved during the summer should reappear the following summer and last for several weeks before changing into their autumn attire.

HOW TO
SELECT
HYDRANGEAS
BY TRAITS

7

Seeking Particular
Plant Characteristics

With macrophyllas, the typical first decision is whether you prefer a mophead or a lacecap. Each flower form offers a great many varieties from which to choose. Once the mophead/lacecap question is settled it is time to think about the traits you would like your selection to offer. The table below lists only six of the hundreds of named varieties in the species with a particular trait noted for each. Keep in mind that many varieties will have more than one trait with some traits more important to you than others. For instance, a variety you are considering might be one that grows well in containers, has good sun tolerance, and dries well. If you plan to plant it not in a container but in a flower bed, and if that flower bed is in dappled shade, the first two traits are irrelevant when you make your decision. It may well be that the only trait you are concerned about is whether the flowers will dry well. If so, this variety is a good choice.

Species	Flower Type	Variety	Trait
macrophylla	mophead	'Masja'	good container plant
macrophylla	mophead	'Merritt's Supreme'	good dried flower
macrophylla	mophead	'Altona'	good for seaside gardens
macrophylla	lacecap	'Lanarth White'	good sun tolerance
macrophylla	lacecap	'Geoffrey Chadbund'	good cut flower
macrophylla	lacecap	'Blaumeise'	large flower heads

It is likely that you are searching for a hydrangea variety that has a cluster of particular traits. Be as clear as you can about what you want. Maybe it is a fairly small lacecap with pink flowers that would thrive in a patio container or a mophead with medium blue flowers that tolerates a lot of sun. Try to identify all the traits that are important to you and prioritize them from most important to least important; doing so will help lead you to the variety that best suits your needs. The more traits you identify, the more you narrow the field. For example, if all you care about is finding a mophead with blue flowers, you will have many varieties from which to choose. If you also want those flowers to dry well, you are narrowing the field. If, on top of that, you want the flower heads to be large you are narrowing the field still more.

When you first notice a variety that appeals to you in a garden setting, recognize that you don't yet know all its traits and, as with people, first impressions can be misleading. The plant you fall in love with might have beautiful large flower heads and if you prefer large flower heads this would be seen as a positive, but it might also have a tendency to flop over in heavy rain which you well might perceive as negative. It is important to become familiar with all of a plant's traits before you decide to add it to your garden. If there are negative traits only you can determine whether the positive traits outweigh them. There might be a lacecap with gorgeous variegated leaves (positive trait) that you know will look perfect next to an existing plant in your garden, but it may be a lacecap that rarely flowers (negative trait). Does the handsome foliage outweigh the lack of flowering? For some gardeners the answer would be yes, and for others, no.

Once you have the full botanical name of a variety you can learn enough about the plant to make an informed decision. Let's say you have just encountered a mophead hydrangea called 'Miss Belgium' in a botanical garden. You love what it looks like. You think you might like to add it to your own garden. Now you should research the plant.

H.m. 'Miss Belgium'.

The easiest way, of course, is by using the various Internet search engines. If you are not computer savvy, do you have a friend, a son, daughter, or grandchild who could help you? Failing the computer route, gardening catalogues can help, but with limitations; they tend to list only the positive traits. The time you invest in tracking down the plant's traits will be well worth it if you end up adding something to your garden that is exactly what you want.

If you researched *Hydrangea macrophylla* 'Miss Belgium' you would learn it is a free-flowering plant about three to four feet tall at maturity with sturdy stems and dark glossy green leaves. The flowers are purple in an acidic soil and a rosy pink in alkaline soil. It flowers in mid-season and the flowers age to deep wine colors. It is a variety that is known to do well in containers. A compact plant, the flower heads

H.m. 'Blaumeise', a lacecap that dries well, attracts the eye with abundant flowers.

Lists of plants with a particular trait (like hydrangeas with flowers that dry well) are compiled as a result of observation by many people in many settings over time. Plants, like people, acquire reputations. As more and more people notice certain traits in their plants, the word spreads until one or more traits are routinely mentioned in their descriptions. This does not mean that you cannot successfully dry the flowers of varieties not in this group. The author has had good luck drying the flowers of many hydrangea varieties not noted for being easy to dry. But again, it is a question of priorities. If the most important thing to you is to be able to dry the flowers then don't take a chance; choose from the varieties recommended as having that trait.

Good dried flowers

Most hydrangea species dry well. If you stagger the harvest of paniculatas you can collect flowers in different colors including medium pink, deep pink, and burgundy. Oakleaf hydrangeas dry in shades of pink, burgundy, and chocolate brown. *Hydrangea arborescens* 'Annabelle' dries green. Most mopheads and lacecaps dry well, especially the following: 'Alpenglühen'; 'Altona'; 'Ayesha'; 'Blaumeise'; 'Bouquet Rose'; 'Deutschland'; 'Enziandom'; 'Europa'; 'Gartenbaudirektor Kühnert'; 'Générale Vicomtesse de

tend to be small, in good proportion to the size of the plant.

These details provide a good amount of helpful information, but suppose you want a mophead variety with flowers that dry well? You have already seen that you like the look of 'Miss Belgium' in the garden and now you have found out it has sturdy stems and that the flowers age to deep wine colors, both positive traits for the dried flowers you have in mind. Your research, however, doesn't answer the question about drying the flowers. Many hydrangea varieties are known for good dried flowers and this trait is noted in their descriptions. What does it mean if the information is *not* noted? Do they not dry well? Are you willing to take a chance? Do you love the plant enough to waive the dried flower requirement if it turns out they don't dry well? Some gardeners would solve the dilemma by adding 'Miss Belgium' to the garden *and* another variety known for flowers that dry well. But you might have space enough for only one plant. This is why it is helpful to prioritize the traits you desire.

Vibraye'; 'Gertrude Glahn'; 'Goliath'; 'Hamburg'; 'Kasteln'; 'King George'; 'Kluis Superba'; 'Lilacina'; 'Madame Faustin Travouillon'; 'Maréchal Foch'; 'Merritt's Supreme'; 'Otaksa'; 'Paris'; 'Princess Beatrix'; 'Princess Juliana', 'Veitchii'; and 'Zaunkönig'.

Good cut flowers

'Altona'; 'Blushing Pink'; 'Böttstein'; 'Bouquet Rose'; 'Deutschland'; 'Enziandom'; 'Europa'; 'Générale Vicomtesse de Vibraye'; 'Geoffrey Chadbund'; 'Hamburg'; 'Kasteln'; 'King George'; 'Kluis Superba'; 'Le Cygne'; 'Madame Faustin Travouillon'; 'Maréchal Foch'; 'Merritt's Supreme'; 'Miss Hepburn'; 'Pink Lace'; 'Princess Beatrix'; 'Princess Juliana'; and 'Tovelit'.

Hydrangeas that work well in containers

Most mopheads and lacecaps can do quite well in a container for an entire summer. Hydrangeas grow quickly, though, and by the end of the summer almost all of them should be transplanted into the garden. The exceptions are the smaller varieties with a tendency to stay compact including 'Adria'; 'Altona'; 'Ami Pasquier'; 'Blauer Zwerg'; 'Blue Danube'; 'Compacta'; 'Forever Pink'; 'Harlequin'; 'Masja'; 'Merritt's Supreme'; Mini Penny™; 'Miss Belgium'; 'Pia'; and 'Pink Lace'.

The mophead 'Ami Pasquier' is one of several varieties known to do well in containers.

Rebloomers

Also called remontant varieties, these hydrangeas will produce flowers on new wood (this season's growth). Until recently

H.m. 'All Summer Beauty', a rebloomer, puts on a good show of flowers all summer long.

all macrophyllas were thought to produce buds on old wood alone. These remontant varieties are of great help to gardeners who live in areas susceptible either to early fall or late spring frosts when flower buds are vulnerable.

Mopheads: 'All Summer Beauty'; 'Blushing Bride'; 'David Ramsey'; 'Decatur Blue'; Endless Summer™; 'Madame Emile Mouillère'; Mini Penny™; 'Oak Hill'; and 'Penny Mac'.

Lacecaps: 'Coerulea Lace'; 'Lanarth White'; 'Lilacina'; and Twist-n-Shout™.

Good for seaside locations

'Altona'; 'Ayesha'; 'Beauté Vendômoise'; 'Blue Wave'; 'Hamburg'; 'La France'; 'La Marne';

H.m. 'Hamburg' not only thrives in seaside gardens, but is also a good cut flower and a good dried flower.

Some hydrangeas are known to be more sun tolerant than others including H.m.'Tokyo Delight' shown here.

'Lanarth White'; 'Madame Emile Mouillère'; 'Otaksa'; 'Seafoam'; and 'Sir Joseph Banks'.

Good sun tolerance

'Altona'; 'Ayesha'; 'Blue Wave'; 'Lanarth White'; 'Lilacina'; 'Otaksa'; and 'Tokyo Delight'.

Large flower heads

Mopheads: 'Altona'; 'Big Daddy'; 'Brestenberg'; 'Europa'; 'Goliath'; 'Kasteln'; 'Kluis Superba'; 'Otaksa'; 'Paris'; and 'Renate Steiniger'.

Lacecaps: 'Beauté Vendômoise'; 'Blue Wave'; 'Pink Lace'; 'Taube'; and 'White Wave'.

Multiple Traits

Some of the better varieties have many features to recommend them. For example, 'Madame Emile Mouillère', is good in containers, has good sun tolerance, flowers abundantly, and is known for repeat flowering, is vigorous and easy to

Hydrangea flowers range widely in size from small to very large. This one, H.m. 'Europa', has large flower heads which are also known to dry well.

These flowers were collected in one Cape Cod garden on the same day. The small mophead at the far left in the front and the large mophead at the far left in the back are both from the same shrub, H.m. 'Dooley'. The smaller flower is more characteristic of the usual size of 'Dooley' flowers; this shrub just happened to produce one exceptionally large flower that season.

The beautiful large flowers of H.m. 'Brestenberg'.

The flowers of H.a. 'Annabelle' are often impressively large.

propagate, and dries well. Michael Dirr calls it "the classic white hydrangea". No wonder it shows up on the list of award winning hydrangea cultivars. (See Chapter Two for award winning hydrangeas.)

Other traits

The traits mentioned above do not constitute an exhaustive list. As you become more acquainted with hydrangeas you will notice qualities in particular varieties that appeal to you and this will make you alert for other examples. It might be the overall structure of the plant, the shape of the flower, or some other distinctive feature. Once it attracts you, you will be on the lookout for others and it can become an enjoyable treasure hunt.

Sometimes you get lucky and find the perfect hydrangea without going through any evaluation process whatsoever. You see a certain variety, you fall in love with it, and you have the perfect spot for it in your garden where it flourishes year after year. All of the previously described strategies are for those who find themselves in the more common situation of thinking *So many beautiful hydrangeas! Which is the right one for me?*

H.m. 'Lemon Wave' with its distinctive variegated foliage.

A dark glossy hydrangea leaf contrasts with the striking chartreuse color of the foliage of H.m. 'Lemon Daddy'.

Some hydrangea varieties have distinctive traits like large eyes, such as those that appear here on H.m. 'Freudenstein'. (The blue "eyes" are centered in the pink flowers.)

H.m. 'Shamrock' has an unusual form.

Does one of these hydrangeas draw your eye first? The answer might provide a clue as to which one is best for you.

MACROPHYLLA

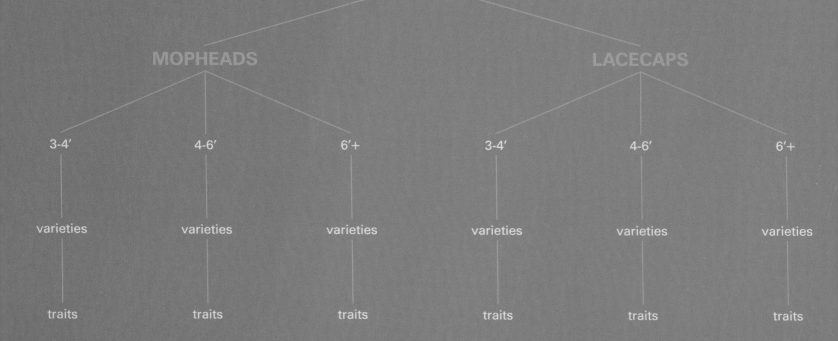

MOPHEADS

3-4′ — varieties — traits

4-6′ — varieties — traits

6′+ — varieties — traits

LACECAPS

3-4′ — varieties — traits

4-6′ — varieties — traits

6′+ — varieties — traits

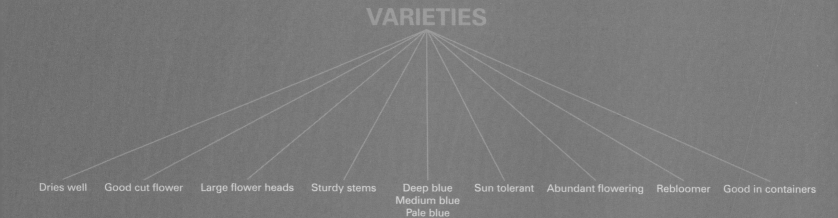

VARIETIES

Dries well | Good cut flower | Large flower heads | Sturdy stems | Deep blue / Medium blue / Pale blue | Sun tolerant | Abundant flowering | Rebloomer | Good in containers

HOW TO PLANT HYDRANGEAS

8

Promoting Good Growing Conditions

When planting close to trees, try to allow several hours of morning sun, with the tree canopy providing afternoon shade.

Where to plant

Before purchasing plants, check to make sure you have the right location. This varies depending on the species.

Macrophyllas (mopheads and lacecaps). The ideal location for this species provides several hours of sunlight, preferably in the morning. Look for a site with an overhead tree canopy as this serves two purposes: afternoon shade and frost protection. A sloping site is good for drainage and also to protect against late frosts; in a sloping site the frost flows away. Evergreens are good companion plants for aesthetic reasons and also for the practical reason that they help to shield the hydrangeas from winter wind. One caution about evergreens: avoid planting hydrangeas near conifers. They tend to absorb most of the available water in the area and their density prevents rain from reaching the hydrangeas. Hollies, on the other hand, are wonderful evergreen companions. The centralized root system of hollies gets water from deep in the ground leaving, water closer to the surface available to the hydrangeas.

Macrophyllas can be planted in full sun but there are drawbacks; the flower color will fade faster and the flowers are more likely to scorch around the edges or completely in harsh afternoon sun. They also require plenty of moisture and it is easier to keep them well hydrated if you protect them from the drying effects of the afternoon sun. Some sun is needed for flowers so don't plant them in deep shade unless all you want from them is healthy foliage.

Summary for macrophyllas: morning sun and afternoon shade.

Paniculatas. In contrast to the mopheads and lacecaps, paniculatas thrive in the sun. Take advantage of sunny spots in your garden by planting one paniculata as a focal point, or mass them together. Paniculatas have brittle stems that can be easily broken in strong winds. If your sunny spot also tends to be very windy,

Paniculatas planted in full sun at a Destelbergen, Belgium, display garden.

consider how you might provide a windbreak.

Summary for paniculatas: sunny sites with wind protection.

Arborescens. Arborescens varieties, of which 'Annabelle' is the most widely planted example, can be planted in full sun in the north, but the further south you go, the less tolerant of sun this species becomes.

As a general guideline for arborescens varieties aim for light shade and consistent moisture.

Quercifolias (oakleaf hydrangeas). Oakleaf hydrangeas are adaptable to either sun or shade. They seem to need plenty of heat to flower well, not surprising since they are natives of the southeastern area of the United States. Flowering is possible in dense shade. These plants are wind sensitive so try to plant them in a sheltered site. The author, who gardens in the moderate summer climate of Cape Cod, had to look around for the right spot for an oakleaf hydrangea. It was planted next to the driveway with its reflected heat, where it gets sun most of the day, and near pine trees which provide protection from the wind. It thrives in this location.

Summary: oakleaf hydrangeas can be planted in either sun or shade, in a sheltered location.

Climbing hydrangeas can thrive in full sun, especially when planted in a northern garden. Here a Cape Cod outdoor shower is camouflaged with climbing hydrangeas.

Climbing hydrangeas. Climbing hydrangeas prefer partial shade but can be planted in full sun. They are remarkably tolerant of poor soil, but, like other hydrangeas, they require good drainage.

In general, climbing hydrangeas prefer partial shade, sufficient moisture and good drainage.

Where *not* to plant

Try not to put a plant in a space that it will inevitably outgrow. It is easy to forget that the nice little compact plant in the two-or three-gallon pot at the garden center might grow to be six feet tall and just as wide (or more). Be aware of the **mature size** of the plant and place it accordingly. This will prevent the later necessity of moving the plant to a better location.

Avoid planting in low spots in the garden which may be pockets of frost during cold weather and which could have drainage problems during the growing season.

Selecting plants at a garden center

When you are new to the world of hydrangeas it is a good idea to go to a reputable garden center to purchase one or more hydrangeas for your garden. Healthy plants will have lots of foliage on a compact frame. You should see plenty of buds and/or flowers. When you lift the plant it should feel heavy, meaning it has been well watered. If you lift a plant and it feels surprisingly light, it may have been allowed to dry out: not good. Actual blooms are better than pictures of blooms so you can see what you are getting. Plants are mislabeled from time to time and it is frustrating to find that out only after one has been planted in your garden.

Once you gain more experience in judging the health of hydrangea plants, you can find some wonderful bargains at discount stores that sell hydrangeas in bulk. Chances are they will not be well labeled to let you know what variety you are looking at. It can be enjoyable to bring them home, plant them, and wait to see what develops, then transplant them to optimum garden arrangement once you see what you have.

Many gardeners like the instant gratification of installing a large plant but keep in mind, a smaller plant will quickly grow to the size of the larger plant. Because the plant is smaller it will suffer less stress when planted as it has fewer blooms and leaves to support.

When to plant

Late spring (after the danger of killing frosts has passed) and fall are both good times of the year for planting. Excessive heat stresses young plants, which is why you should avoid planting during the heat of the summer if at all possible. If you must plant during the summer, try for early morning on a calm day when cool weather is forecast for at least several days. You want to give your plant a chance to settle in without struggling against high daytime temperatures. Some gardeners will try to minimize the harmful effects of strong sunlight and excessive heat by positioning garden umbrellas over the plants for a few weeks to give them time to settle in.

When *not* to plant

Try to avoid planting when such unfavorable conditions as excessive heat or high winds are present. The newly planted hydrangeas will be stressed under these conditions. Similarly avoid periods of frost or drought. Resist the temptation to get the plant in the ground as soon

as possible. It can do very nicely in a container in a sheltered area until conditions improve.

How to Plant

Before digging the hole, water the plant in its container. You want it to be nice and moist before placing it in its new location.

The ideal soil for hydrangeas is rich with organic material, moist but not overly wet, and drains well. If your garden has heavy clay soil you might want to amend the soil with compost, shredded leaves, well-rotted manure and other organic materials. If your soil is sandy, amending with organic materials will help supply nutrients and retain moisture.

Dig a hole that is twice the diameter of the plant in the pot. Your goal is to have the top surface of the soil in the plant match the surface of the ground in which it is planted. It will struggle if planted too deeply.

When you remove it from the pot, loosen the roots as much as you can without causing all the soil to fall away. You might have to be a little rougher with a root-bound plant. The goal is to have roots spread out in such a way that the plant will adapt to its new environment easily. Fill in around it with rich soil, pressing down as you go to remove air pockets. Once you have completed filling in with soil all around the plant until the filled-in soil matches the ground

level around it, water it in well. The final step is to add mulch around the plant (but not pressing against its base) to help retain moisture in the soil and to discourage weeds.

Don't worry if you don't see many flowers the first few years the plant is in the ground. The young plant is devoting its energy to growth, getting itself established with a healthy root system. Once this is accomplished, the plant will reward your patience with beautiful blooms.

Transplanting

Reasons for transplanting vary. Changing conditions in your garden often create the need to move plants around. A mophead planted under a small tree might get sufficient sunlight at first but when the tree grows and the shade is more dense the mophead will tell you it needs to move by producing leaves only, with no flowers. Another hydrangea might outgrow its location. Trees might be damaged and have to be removed, leaving some afternoon shade-loving mopheads in the full sun. Sometimes when you purchase a home with an established garden you want to move plants around for aesthetic reasons. Fortunately hydrangeas can be moved successfully as long as you understand their needs.

With shallow roots and an unfussy nature, most hydrangeas are easy to transplant. By taking a few minimal precautions you will

The hydrangeas in the foreground of this Cape Cod garden were originally planted under a canopy provided by two tall pine trees. When the pine trees became diseased and had to be removed the hydrangea shrubs showed signs of stress the first summer they were exposed to full sun all day. Transplanting was considered, but they subsequently adapted to the new conditions.

find your hydrangea adapting fairly quickly to its new environment. Timing is important. It is better for the plant if it is moved in its dormant state. How to tell when it is dormant? Wait until all the leaves have fallen off and transplant it before fresh green growth appears in the spring. The exact month you do this will depend on where you live and whether the ground is frozen when you want to move your plant(s). November would generally be a good time for transplanting hydrangeas in the northeast, before the ground freezes. Further south you may be able to wait until December or even later if it is an especially mild winter.

This is not to say you cannot transplant hydrangeas at other times of the year; it is just less stressful for the plant to do it while it is dormant. If you choose to move a hydrangea

during the growing season, you should take some steps to minimize stress. One thing you can do is cut the plant back before moving it. Depending on the time of year you do this you might be removing some of next year's flowers but that is a small price to pay to keep the plant healthy and viable. You should finish digging a new hole and amending the soil in the new area before digging up the plant and moving it to its new location. Have a tarp handy. The roots are shallow and may be as wide as the branch system, so try to dig up as much of the root system as possible.

Once the plant is dug up, you can place it on the tarp and drag it to the new spot. All of this should be done in a cool part of the day, morning or evening, and preferably when cooler weather is in the forecast for a few days. A rainy week can be depressing for people who want to go to the beach but perfect for the gardener who wants to move hydrangeas around. As soon as you have finished transplanting, make sure you water it in well, and check moisture levels regularly over the next few weeks.

Moisture needs of young plants

The newly installed plant, whether just planted for the first time or transplanted, is yet to establish the good root system

required for easily supporting both foliage and large blossoms. During the first few years you should pay careful attention to its need for water, especially during dry spells or on windy days.

A lacecap hydrangea planted in ideal conditions in a North Carolina garden. It receives several hours of morning sun, is shielded from the harsher afternoon sun, and has been placed so that it receives the benefit of rainwater gushing from the downspout. Mulch helps the soil retain moisture and the surrounding holly shrubs provide additional protection.

A raised bed near Hyannis Harbor on Cape Cod provides excellent drainage, but care needs to be taken to assure sufficient moisture.

HOW TO PROVIDE BASIC CARE

9

Nurturing Your Hydrangeas Through the Seasons

A neglected hydrangea in the yard of a dilapidated house still manages to look beautiful.

Fortunately for those of us who love them, hydrangeas are low maintenance plants. A little bit of effort in feeding and watering goes a long way toward producing healthy shrubs bearing lush blooms. Gardeners think in terms of seasons and this chapter is organized to reflect that. Advice on how to care for your hydrangeas in spring, summer, fall, and winter should help you focus on the basic needs of your hydrangeas in each season.

Light pruning is needed to remove old flowers and dead wood.

The pruning takes just a few minutes and the plant looks much better.

Six weeks after the light springtime pruning, an abundant flower display begins.

Spring Care

This general cleanup time is the perfect time to do a light pruning, fertilize your plants, pull weeds, and apply mulch.

Lightly prune. Remove old flower heads. Cut bare sticks down to fresh green growth. Remove crossed branches and dead wood. (If unsure if a stem is dead just scratch it lightly to see if you find green just beneath the surface. If you see green, the stem is still alive.) By the time the light pruning is done the shrub should look essentially the same in size, just cleaned up. Take care not to cut branches back severely as this would remove some buds for this year's flowers.

Fertilize. An easy way to feed hydrangeas is to apply a balanced, time-released fertilizer (like Osmocote) in early spring. Other forms of fertilizers require frequent applications, some as often as once every two weeks, whereas the time-release forms can provide nutrients for up to three months. In any case, check the package directions for recommended quantity and frequency of application. If using the granular time-released type, make sure the soil is moist when applying it, and be careful to apply it to the soil only and not to the foliage as it could burn the foliage. No matter what the frequency rate, make sure the first application is in early spring to give your plants a good start for the growing season. Well-nourished plants tend to be healthy plants. Healthy plants are better able to resist diseases and stresses caused by environmental conditions like drought.

If using a time-released fertilizer, make note of when you apply it so that you will know when to apply more fertilizer in the summer. If the one you apply says it provides nutrients for three months, make a note on your calendar when that three month period expires.

A balanced fertilizer, such as one with an NPK ratio of 10/10/10, provides equal proportions of nitrogen, phosphorous, and potassium. (N=nitrogen, P=phosphorous, K=potassium). This is a good all-purpose fertilizer and is fine for all hydrangeas. But if you particularly want your flowers to be blue or pink, different NPK ratios are recommended.

If blue flowers are desired, apply a nitrate-based fertilizer with an NPK ratio of 25/5/30. Nitrate-based is recommended because nitrates are released slowly. The alternative is ammonium-based which is not recommended because it acts quickly and by using it you risk burning the roots.

Phosphorous tends to block the absorption of aluminum. Hydrangeas need to absorb aluminum for blue flowers. The middle number in the ratio (the "P" in NPK), represents phosphorous, therefore you want that number to be low if blue flowers are desired. Bone meal and superphosphates also block the absorption of aluminum so avoid the use of these products if you want blue flowers.

An annual application of **aluminum sulfate** will further help develop the best blue possible but be careful with the amounts you use. ***Too much aluminum sulfate can be toxic to the plants***. Follow package directions carefully. There is a danger in thinking if some is good, some more must be better. If the package directions say to add one tablespoon of aluminum sulfate to one gallon of water, that is the safe amount to use. Adding more of the product to the same amount of water could hurt your plant instead of making the flowers develop stronger color.

If pink flowers are desired, apply a nitrate-based fertilizer with an NPK ratio of 25/10/10. Also add lime to the soil twice a year. Dolomite lime is best, following package directions. Lime raises the pH of the soil resulting in a more alkaline soil in which you are more likely to get pink flowers than blue flowers. Don't go overboard with the lime. Too much lime applied at any one time can cause chlorosis, an iron deficiency. (Yellow leaves are a symptom of chlorosis.)

No matter what fertilizer you are using, make sure you water it in well, to help it get down to the roots. Fertilizing on a day when rain is in the forecast is a good idea.

Apply mulch. Once you have weeded around your shrubs, apply two inches of mulch which helps in two ways: mulch discourages further weeds from taking root in the area and also keeps the soil evenly moist, a desirable condition for hydrangeas. Do not pile mulch up around the base of the plant.

Summer Care

When your hydrangeas start to bloom see that as a sign that they now need lots of food and water. They can absorb nutrients and water rapidly, not surprising when you consider the size of the flowers and foliage. Watering will be a major concern throughout the summer and a summer feed is essential to keep your plants as healthy as possible.

Water. Hydrangeas need a lot of water but they don't like to be waterlogged. Soil with good drainage is essential. Loose, nutrient rich soil is ideal. Heavy clay soils are particularly challenging. If you notice water standing on the surface for any length of time, you may have to improve the drainage by digging up the plant, amending the soil and replanting.

A system of soaker hoses surrounding hydrangea plants. Once the soaker hoses were in place the area was mulched to help retain moisture.

Raised beds like this provide excellent drainage. Extra water may be needed on particularly hot and/or windy days.

The roots of hydrangeas need air as well as water. Deprived of air (in a too dense, wet soil) the plant can develop root rot. Avoid planting hydrangeas in low lying areas of the garden where water tends to accumulate.

Presuming you have planted your hydrangeas in a naturally good soil, or have amended the soil to improve conditions, the watering requirements are simple. Keep this goal in mind: hydrangeas thrive in consistently moist (not overly wet) soil. A drip irrigation system is ideal with water being released slowly and consistently.

Overhead sprinkler systems help provide the necessary water, but too much of it goes to the leaves (sometimes causing spotting) when it would be better for the health of the plant if all the water were directed to the roots. If you water with a hose, direct the water to the base of the plant. Early morning watering is best. It is better for the plant to be deeply watered once a week than to receive a little water every day, because it forces the roots deeper in the soil as they seek moisture. As stated above, mulch will help the plant retain moisture which can be very important on hot summer days.

Note that hydrangeas in containers and raised beds need more frequent watering than those in normal garden beds. When in doubt, stick your finger into the soil to make sure it is not dry beneath the surface.

Hint: If you are going to be away from your garden for several days and you don't have a sprinkler system, you can make use of gallon size plastic milk jugs or two-liter size plastic bottles to improvise a soaker system. Poke small holes in the bottom of the plastic containers, fill them with water, cap them, and place them at the base of hydrangea plants. The water will seep slowly into the surrounding soil.

Summer fertilizer. Foliage on your hydrangea can tell you a lot about its fertilizer needs. If your hydrangea has lush and healthy foliage but few flowers it may be a sign you are over-fertilizing. Fertilizers with a high nitrogen content (the "N" in the NPK ratio) can produce lots of leaves at the expense of flowers.

Yellowing leaves on the inside of a hydrangea shrub is the first sign of a nutrient deficiency, usually a nitrogen and/or iron deficiency. Applying fertilizer will address that problem.

Fall Care

Watering should continue in the fall and this is also the time of year to consider cutting some flowers to dry. If your soil is not ideal, this is a good time to add two inches of compost around your shrubs. Avoid fertilizing your hydrangeas in the fall as this leads to new growth which is tender and susceptible to damage from harsh winter conditions.

Dry flowers. Fall is the time to harvest hydrangea blooms to dry. You can tell the flowers are ready for this if they feel papery. They have probably already faded to their antique colors when they are ready to be dried. See Chapter 16 for detailed advice on drying hydrangeas.

Apply compost. Skip this step if your soil is already well amended. If your soil quality is less than ideal, fall is a good time to add two inches of compost around your plants.

Remove cuttings to a protected area. If you have taken cuttings to propagate your plant(s), late fall is the best time to move them to a protected area for the winter months. See Chapter 14 for details on propagation and protected areas.

Winter Care

If you live in a cold climate (zone 6 and below), some protection will be required for your hydrangeas so they will survive winter and bloom the following summer. You need to wait until the plants have become dormant before applying winter protection. Use the foliage as a guide. When all the leaves have fallen off the plant, it is time to apply protection. Your goal is to

This whimsical representation of winter protection is a little misleading because the protection shouldn't be applied until dormancy when all leaves have fallen off the shrub(s).

provide an environment that will protect the stems and buds from harsh temperatures and fierce winter winds that can dry out the flower buds.

One way to do this is to surround the plant with chicken wire to a level slightly higher than the plant. Make sure the wire is secured at ground level so that it won't tip over, and around its circumference so that it won't split apart. Now fill in around the plant with pine needles or leaves. Pine needles are preferable because they don't pack down as much as leaves during the winter. The protection should be removed when all danger of frost is past and fresh green growth appears on the plants. The average last frost date varies from one region

of the country to another. When in doubt, consult your local master gardeners or a staff member at a garden center.

If you live in zones 7-9, some, but not all, hydrangeas should be protected. Young plants (those put in the ground in the last two years) would do well with protection. The more mature the plant, the hardier it becomes. Florist hydrangeas (the ones sold at Easter and Mother's Day, for instance) are tender plants and should be protected for several years until they become hardened off. Container plants (like those you grow in a large pot on the deck all summer) should be removed to a protected area for the winter; an unheated basement, a garage, or a garden shed could be used for this purpose.

If a hard freeze is forecast after a spring thaw, the flower buds on your mopheads and lacecaps are in jeopardy. This situation calls for temporary protection which may only be necessary for a few nights. Frost sheets can be placed over your plants (and secured so wind doesn't cause them to fly off) and left in place for a few days. Frost sheets are designed to let the plants breathe. If your local garden center doesn't stock frost sheets you can cover your plants overnight with household sheets and blankets; just make sure you remove these during the day when temperatures rise to above

freezing. You don't want to smother your plants. Plastic is not a good material for winter protection; it could cause more harm than good.

Late winter pruning. This is a good time to cut back your hydrangeas that bloom on new wood: the paniculatas and arborescens.

Ease of maintenance. Considering the impressively long season of bloom and the powerful presence even just one hydrangea shrub can have in the garden, the work required to keep them healthy is minimal. Prune them lightly in the late winter or early spring. Feed them in the early spring. Keep the soil moist. Mulch to help retain moisture. Enjoy all summer with very little additional effort. Hydrangeas can be vigorous and healthy for decades if you provide this kind of basic care. It is simple, it takes very little time, and it is worth it.

Summary

Spring

- Lightly prune
- Fertilize
- Pull weeds
- Apply mulch

Summer

- Water
- Fertilize again, as needed
- Prune mopheads and lacecaps immediately after flowering

Fall

- Continue watering
- Harvest for dried flowers
- Apply compost
- Remove cuttings to protected area

Winter

- Protect tender plants
- Prune paniculatas and arborescens in late winter

HOW TO INCORPORATE HYDRANGEAS INTO YOUR GARDEN DESIGN

10

Landscaping with Hydrangeas

With the wide range of plants in the hydrangea world it is easy to find varieties to fit your landscaping plans. If bloom time is a consideration, you can have hydrangeas in bloom from early spring with the climbing hydrangeas, throughout the summer with mopheads, lacecaps, arborescens and oakleaf hydrangeas, and well into fall with the paniculatas.

Most hydrangeas are happy in partial shade but can survive in full sun and, in the case of paniculatas, thrive in full sun. Many hydrangeas do well in containers, allowing for even more flexibility of placement.

Hydrangeas can be used as foundation plantings, hedges, focal points, and as a textured tapestry of color along driveways and fences. Flower colors are available to suit all tastes including blue, pink, purple, white, cream, and green.

Placing hydrangeas where they can be seen from windows in the house takes advantage of the long blooming season. The flowers not only look wonderful during their peak season, but also age to soft antique shades.

Hydrangeas require very little maintenance and survive for many years in the home landscape relatively untroubled by pests or diseases. They provide peak performance under ideal conditions and still look very good under less-than-ideal conditions. Hydrangeas found near abandoned properties often look just as healthy as those on well-tended properties.

There are dwarf hydrangeas for containers and small gardens, and dramatically large hydrangeas for more accommodating spaces. Some hydrangeas provide notable fall color, especially the oakleaf hydrangeas.

Because the world of hydrangeas offers over 1200 varieties, the possibilities for the home gardener are extensive and growing more so each year as their popularity increases. All it takes is to see one mophead in a color you love, or one lacecap with a flowerhead the size of a dinner plate or one paniculata

dramatically taking center stage in a large space for you to realize you want that mophead and that lacecap and that paniculata in your own garden. You will find space for them. And then you will want more.

Masses of Hydrangeas

Hydrangeas are wonderfully effective in the landscape when massed together. It is purely a matter of the gardener's personal preference whether the mass should be all the same variety, creating a uniform look, or multiple varieties creating a more textured look. Some people mass their mopheads, but use single

A mass of *Hydrangea arborescens* Incrediball™ in a Cape Cod garden.

Blue mopheads peeking through a fence on the island of Martha's Vineyard.

paniculatas as focal points. Others mass paniculatas as hedges or at the back of the yard marking the property line. A white garden could feature masses of white lacecaps in one area, white mopheads in a second area, *Hydrangea arborescens* 'Annabelle' in a third area, and the paniculata 'Limelight' in a fourth area, thus creating a garden with substantial white impact in spring, summer, and fall.

Accenting

Existing Features

Fences and hydrangeas go together beautifully. Somehow the rigid symmetry of fences juxtaposed with the bouncy abandon of hydrangeas enhances the beauty of each. Look at any fence on your property with a critical eye and imagine it graced with a profusion of blue mopheads or the giant white

A tapestry of mopheads in Edgartown, Martha's Vineyard.

The angles of this pink house are softened with the mass of mainly pink mopheads in a front flower bed.

Mounding hydrangea shrubs, with their large round flowers, echo the rounded arches of the house and garden gate.

A mass of paniculatas ('Limelight') at the entrance of Heritage Museums and Gardens, Sandwich, Massachusetts.

These fairly young hydrangeas will grow larger in the following years providing plenty of blue mopheads for visual pleasure around this lovely Cape Cod porch.

Locate hydrangeas where they can be seen from inside a house

pom-pom flowers of *H.arborescens* 'Annabelle'. The flowers will soften the fence. The fence will support the flowers. They are a good match.

Striking **architectural features** of a house or a small free-standing structure on a property (such as a gazebo, pergola, and garden shed) can be made even more attractive with the right hydrangea as an accent. Less attractive features can be camouflaged. Climbing hydrangeas planted at the base of a chain link fence will soften the effect of that fence turning it, eventually, into a thing of beauty.

The sunroom of a charming Cape Cod house frequently visited by the author is a hydrangea lover's delight. No matter which windows you look through, you see beautiful displays of hydrangeas. Look out the windows on the right side and enjoy the humorous sight of the giant white flowers of *H.a.* 'Annabelle' appearing to peek in the windows. The windows overlooking the back garden provide a perfect view of a row of 'Tardiva' paniculatas. The French door on the left leads to a patio surrounded by mopheads, lacecaps and a wonderful assortment

The cheerful white flowers of *Hydrangea arborescens* 'Annabelle' outside a Cape Cod sunroom.

of companion plants. The garden in the back is a hydrangea wonderland that can be enjoyed from both inside and outside the house.

A planned view can sometimes provide an unexpected bonus. The author planted a climbing hydrangea at the base of a tree that is easily seen from a bay window at the back of the house. Once the vine was well established it was a treat to see the white blossoms covering the tree in early spring. Once the flowers had gone by, the tree was less of a focal point until fall when the foliage turned yellow. On a day when morning fog filled the garden the tree was a pillar of glowing yellow, resembling a giant candle glowing in the mist. The sight was ethereal and priceless, the unexpected bonus of planting that climbing hydrangea where it could be seen easily from the house.

Ideal locations for hydrangeas are outside a kitchen window where a sink is located, outside low dining room windows, and outside bedroom windows where beautiful hydrangeas can be the first things seen every morning; a good way to start the day.

Locate hydrangeas near entryways

Locating hydrangeas near entryways makes it easy for the resident to get nice close views of the beautiful flowers regularly. It also makes it easier to snip a few blooms for an indoor arrangement when desired.

Some gardeners who love the look of hydrangeas at the front of a house but are unhappy with the off-season appearance, use hydrangeas

Purple mopheads appear above evergreen shrubs at the front entry of a Cape Cod house.

in pots at the front of the house. These can be whisked away to a hidden location when the flowers have passed their prime. Another solution is to plant hydrangeas behind evergreen shrubs that can be pruned to be slightly shorter than the hydrangeas. In this way the hydrangea flowers can be enjoyed from the street yet in the winter when the hydrangea shrub looks more like a collection of tall sticks, that view is hidden behind the evergreen shrub in front of it.

Companion Plants

Successful gardeners understand the concept of companion planting; they group certain plants together that look good in their own right and also enhance each other by virtue of being close together. (All the plants involved would require

Blue mopheads and pink roses are a classic combination in a Cape Cod garden.

The colors of the flowers in the window box really stand out vividly over the skirt provided by the giant white blooms of *Hydrangea arborescens* 'Annabelle'.

Mounding evergreens complement this mounding mophead hydrangea.

Deep pink roses perfectly accent the dark blue flowers of these mopheads.

The pink flowers of 'Preziosa' contrast nicely with surrounding grasses.

A classic blue and white effect with blue lacecaps and daisies.

A scene in Wales where pure white paniculata flowers stand out against an evergreen background.

similar growing conditions.) You will, no doubt, already have favorite combinations of your own. Hydrangeas combine well with a wide variety of plants. The suggestions provided below do not constitute an exhaustive list but represent some tried-and-true combinations. An easy way for you to discover wonderful combinations in your own garden is to plant a hydrangea in a container and move it around the garden all summer, looking to see what combinations work best.

Some combinations work not because they flower at the same time but because they work well in the garden together. If you underplant mopheads and lacecaps with small spring bulbs you will have the beauty of the spring flowering bulbs visible before the hydrangeas leaf out. Once they leaf out, the spent flowers and yellowing foliage of the bulbs are hidden from sight.

Note: Not all combinations work in every climate. For example, daylilies are frequently paired with mopheads in northern climates where the mopheads can be sited in full sun; in southern climates this wouldn't work at all.

Suggested combinations

Hydrangeas with astilbe (There are many good
    color combinations possible.)
Hydrangeas with hostas
Deep pink mopheads with soft pink geraniums
Medium pink mopheads with yellow begonias
Hydrangeas with all kinds of evergreens
Hydrangeas with magnolia
Hydrangeas with holly
Hydrangeas with such groundcovers
    as ivy or vinca
'Annabelle' hydrangeas and 'Frosty Morn' sedum
'Annabelle' hydrangeas and
    Spirea japonica
Mophead hydrangeas with
    'Autumn Joy' sedum
Hydrangeas and campanulas
Blue mophead hydrangeas with
    yellow daylilies

Blue mopheads with *Alchemilla mollis*
    (Lady's Mantle)
Blue mopheads with 'The Fairy' rose
H. *paniculata* 'Limelight' with 'Lime Frost' daylilies

Different hydrangea species as companions for each other

Because there is such a wide variety of form and color in the hydrangea world it is easy to find different varieties that look good together. When you look at the hydrangeas for sale in garden centers, certain combinations will suggest themselves to you.

The big white flowers of *Hydrangea arborescens* 'Annabelle' can be paired with many varieties and colors of *Hydrangea macrophylla*. As they age the Annabelles will turn green and the mopheads will soften to antique shades, and these, too, look lovely together.

Most hydrangeas complement each other as in this garden where white oakleaf flowers, purple and pink mopheads, and blue mopheads lead the eye to the garden arch.

Hydrangea arborescens 'Annabelle' (background) with the mophead variety called 'Harlequin' (foreground).

Hydrangea paniculata 'Limelight' with the blue flowers of Endless Summer®.

Mopheads soften a stone wall.

Lovely lacecaps amid beautifully textured landscaping along a Martha's Vineyard driveway.

A horse barn in rural Plymouth, Massachusetts, is framed by the dramatic white flowers of *Hydrangea paniculata* 'Limelight'.

A paniculata tree framing a water view at a Cape Cod golf course.

These paniculatas outside the library in Sandwich, Massachusetts, seem to be aspiring to literary heights.

These mopheads are just the right height to create a lovely effect with the window boxes at a Nantucket home.

White mopheads complement blue or purple mopheads. Try 'Sister Theresa' (white) with 'Niedersachen'.

Mopheads and lacecaps can be combined effectively, especially when complementary colors are woven together in a kind of tapestry effect. If you choose colors of different intensity, you give the grouping a beautiful depth of color, for instance, pale pink combined with medium pink and deep pink.

Paniculatas can be paired with either mopheads or lacecaps. A paniculata pruned into tree form could have a ring of mopheads or lacecaps at its base.

Hydrangeas are a wonderful addition to the home landscape. They provide accents in varied heights and look good in both formal and informal settings. They can be used to frame a view, soften the effect of a hard material, and provide long-lasting color.

HOW TO GROW HYDRANGEAS IN CONTAINERS

11

Increasing Planting Options

A window box filled with potted hydrangeas in early May on Beacon Hill in Boston, Massachusetts.

If your garden cannot accommodate hydrangeas for whatever reason (wrong climate zone, too much shade, limited planting space, etc.) don't despair; you can always grow hydrangeas in containers. The author has spotted hydrangeas in window boxes on Beacon Hill in Boston, in an exceptionally large pot in an Atlanta garden, and in various containers outside the famed Ritz Hotel in London. Hydrangeas can look at home in both casual and formal settings and can be used to accent front doors, add color to decks and patios, and fill the empty garden spots that occur when perennials fade away. Once you start filling containers with hydrangeas you will continually find more uses for them.

Reasons for Growing Hydrangeas in Containers

Four common reasons for growing hydrangeas in containers rather than directly in the garden are:

- to allow flexibility of placement
- to counteract limited gardening space
- to avoid poor conditions for hydrangeas in the garden
- to control for flower color

A cluster of containers on a small entry porch allows an interplay of pink impatiens, the pink mophead 'Princess Beatrix', and the chartreuse foliage of the hydrangea called 'Lemon Daddy'.

Flexibility of placement. Plants in containers can be placed anywhere you desire. If the only gardening space you have is a patio or deck, you can still grow hydrangeas and enjoy their wonderful blooms all summer long.

Displaying hydrangeas in containers can bring the lovely blooms up to eye level anywhere in the garden.

Hydrangea macrophylla 'Ayesha' in a downtown Nantucket window box.

Hydrangeas in pots are wonderful fillers for those inevitable gaps in the garden when perennials have faded away. They can be moved into position as needed.

Hydrangeas in pots can camouflage an unsightly area in your yard. It doesn't take many to do the job since they are so lush and full.

When hydrangeas are grown in containers they can be used for special effects. Rows of white hydrangeas, for instance, can line either side of an aisle for an outdoor wedding. Large pots of blue hydrangeas placed around a swimming pool echo the color of the water and create a cooling effect.

Some people place containers on bases with wheels so they can be moved around an area (like a deck) easily. This leads to even greater flexibility of placement.

Limited gardening space. If your garden is located in a small space such as a patio, deck, rooftop, or small courtyard, you can use hydrangeas in pots to good effect. Paniculatas can provide important vertical elements, while mopheads offer lush color at a lower level. Variety in form can be achieved by pairing mopheads with lacecaps. Whites, blues, purples, and pinks can be intermixed to suit your color scheme. With proper care, your hydrangeas can be in bloom for several months. The end result is big impact for relatively little effort.

A single mophead with big impact on this Atlanta, Georgia, patio.

Poor Conditions for Hydrangeas in the Garden

Too much shade. Most hydrangeas need at least partially sunny conditions to bloom. If your garden is in dense shade, your hydrangeas could be very healthy with lovely foliage, but they won't produce the magnificent blooms for which they are known. Containers, preferably those that are easy to move, allow you to take advantage of any sun available. If the containers themselves are not easy to move you can put them in a cart of some sort, something you can wheel around easily; a moveable feast for the eyes.

Too much sun. Lack of sunshine isn't the only condition detrimental to hydrangeas. Too much sun can cause a different kind of problem. Hydrangeas will grow well in full sun but intense afternoon sun can crisp the blooms around the edges. If your intent is to dry the blooms at the end of the season, the resulting crop would be unsightly under these conditions. Hydrangea varieties that dry well could be planted in containers and placed in more favorable conditions: morning sun and afternoon shade.

Soil too wet. If your garden is very wet, you could have a problem with most plants. Poor drainage is a major problem leading to root rot and the eventual death of hydrangeas. Planting them in containers with good drainage solves that problem nicely.

The desire to control the color. A hydrangea grower in Oregon had previously worked in California

Pink hydrangea blooms will remain pink in a container when planted in most commercial potting soils. The same hydrangea planted in acidic soil would eventually produce blue flowers, after going through gradual color changes.

where hydrangea lovers wondered what they could do to achieve blue hydrangeas in their gardens. Their alkaline soil produced pinks and reds, but not blues. He moved to Oregon where blues thrive and found people wondering how to produce glorious pinks and reds. Pining for something different seems to be part of that *grass is always greener on the other side of the fence* philosophy. Applying doses of aluminum sulfate (for blue flowers) or lime (for pink or red flowers) is an option, but it involves another step in gardening chores and takes time to achieve the desired results. A much easier way to have the colors you desire is to plant the hydrangeas in containers in neutral soil such as the kind found in a commercial potting mix. Pinks will occur naturally. If blues are desired it is a simple matter to add aluminum sulfate to the soil in a container.

Commercial soil mixes tend to be neither acidic nor alkaline, but neutral. Most hydrangeas tend to produce pink flowers in a neutral soil. This is why you can see rows of 'Nikko Blue' mopheads in containers at a garden center sporting all pink flowers. When you plant them in an acidic soil they will eventually produce the blue tones for which they were named. **Note:** White hydrangeas remain white; they are unaffected by the pH of the soil.

It follows, then, that if it is a pink hydrangea you want to grow in a container, you are in luck. Plant it in the container and pink is what you will get. If the intensity of pink is important to you, you must select a variety with the intensity of color you desire. Pale pinks will always be pale; there is nothing you can add to the soil to make it a richer, deeper pink. If blue is what you want, you will need to add aluminum sulfate to the soil. This is available in powder form in garden centers. Take care in using this additive, since too much of it can be toxic to hydrangeas. The directions usually advise using a certain specified quantity per gallon of water. Check the recommended ratio on the product you purchase. Apply this to the soil in the container at regular intervals early in the growing season. Water in well and allow at least two weeks between applications.

Proper Care of Hydrangeas in Containers

A hydrangea planted in a garden bed with good soil, proper drainage, and sufficient water will pretty much take care of itself. Not so the hydrangeas in a container. While not overly fussy or temperamental, it still has special requirements that must be met in order for it to thrive. Attention should be paid to these variables: size of container; drainage; planting mix; water; and food.

Garden centers often offer large hydrangea shrubs in containers of an appropriate size. Oversized container plantings are sought after for instant impact in the garden.

You may vary the height of containers to create pleasing effects.

Ideal container. The container should be **large enough** to support the plant's growth. When in doubt, ask for advice at a garden center. If you live in a cold climate you should also consider where you will overwinter the container and plan its size accordingly. If the container is too heavy or unwieldy for you to move, you could have a problem, unless you plan to transplant to a more manageable container for the winter.

The container you select should have at least one hole at the bottom for **drainage**. Some gardeners improve drainage by placing various objects like pieces of broken crockery in the bottom of the pot before adding the planting mix. The goal is to allow excess water to flow out easily. Hydrangeas that become waterlogged develop root rot so make sure your container has good drainage for the health of the plant.

A light colored container is better than a dark color because the **light color** will reflect heat away from the roots of the plant. Hydrangeas thrive in a temperate climate so it is important to keep the soil evenly moist and on the cool side. **Mulch** on the surface will help with these goals as well.

Planting mix. Garden soil is generally too dense for containers, particularly if it is a heavy clay soil. Garden soil doesn't drain well enough to withstand the frequent watering required for plants in containers. Good quality commercial potting mixes allow for good drainage and are light enough for roots to grow easily.

How to plant. Place several inches of potting soil in the bottom of the container, center the plant on top of that, and fill in around the plant with more potting soil. Try to keep the plant centered and upright with one hand while filling in with the other. Firm the soil gently with your hand. This will help eliminate any air pockets that may have formed. When the plant is firmly in place, top with a layer of mulch and water well.

Water. Because hydrangeas like a lot of water there is a belief that you can't water a hydrangea too much. This is incorrect. You want the soil in the container to be light and moist, not sopping wet. Overly wet soil leads to root rot, and when the roots start rotting away they are no longer able to take in the amount of oxygen needed for survival. Clearly you don't want your hydrangeas to suffocate. A plant suffering from root rot starts to wilt and, unfortunately, wilting provokes most gardeners into watering more, which hastens the plant's demise.

It is best to water at the base of the plant, directing the water to the roots and not to the flowers and foliage. A soaker system is ideal.

Now don't get nervous about watering; just be aware that enough is enough. So how much is enough? A thorough watering once a day is generally sufficient. You may have heard that container plants should be watered twice a day, but this advice refers to hanging plants on very hot or windy days when they tend to dry out more quickly. If you are in doubt about whether you are supplying enough water, stick your finger into the soil as far as it will go. If the soil is dry just under the surface, you either haven't watered enough or the soil dried out completely at some point which caused it to shrink away from the sides of the pot. When this happens all the watering you do rushes down the sides without moistening the soil. If this is the case you need to submerge the plant completely in water until the soil relaxes enough to absorb the necessary moisture.

Food. All the watering mentioned above has the positive effect of providing sufficient moisture. Unfortunately it also has the negative effect of leaching nutrients from the soil. If you want your container plants to thrive, you must feed them.

Fertilizer choices can be very confusing. They can take the form of time-release granules (like Osmocote), or a powder to be mixed with water (such as Miracle-Gro), or a commercial potting mix that has been pre-mixed with fertilizer. The bottom line is you get to choose *how* you feed your plants but feed them you must, somehow, if you want them to thrive in containers.

Notice the word "thrive" in the previous sentence. It is possible for plants to survive for a while when they are deprived of nutrients, but they become weak (as we would be when deprived of food) and more susceptible to disease and pests. It is much better to keep them healthy and vigorous and they will reward you by looking their best, which is very good indeed.

When you choose a fertilizer for blue hydrangeas, look for one that is low in phosphorus because phosphorus reduces the ability of the plant to absorb aluminum (which makes the flower blue). In the NPK designation, "P" stands for phosphorus, so you will want to make sure that number is low. The recommended NPK ratio for blues is 25/5/30. For pinks and reds: 25/10/10.

Overwintering. Hydrangeas planted in the garden are able to survive cold winters by going dormant. Hydrangeas in containers will also go dormant but that doesn't mean you can leave them outside. The soil in the pot is vulnerable to winter cold and will likely freeze in which case the roots of the hydrangea will no longer be able to breathe and the plant will die. You need to bring potted hydrangeas to a sheltered place for the winter. Ideal locations are unheated garages, sheds and basements where the cold temperature allows the plant to go dormant, but not so cold that the soil will freeze. Temperatures in the forties are very good for this purpose.

Your overwintered hydrangeas will need to be watered but not very much and not very often. The amount of watering depends on the size of the pot. The author successfully overwintered potted cuttings in four-inch pots in an unheated basement, watering them once every two weeks with a tiny amount of water each time (maybe three tablespoons). Naturally a large plant would need more water. Good judgment is needed, but keep in mind, too much water leads to root rot. It is better for them to be more on the dry side than the wet side.

Hydrangea Varieties Recommended for Containers

MOPHEADS AND LACECAPS

'Adria'; 'Altona'; 'Ami Pasquier'; 'Blauer Zwerg'; 'Blue Danube'; 'Compacta'; 'Forever Pink'; 'Harlequin'; 'Hörnli'; 'Masja'; 'Merritt's Supreme'; Mini Penny™; 'Miss Belgium'; 'Pia'; 'Pink Lace'; 'Tovelit'; and all varieties in the Cityline™ (Berlin, Paris, Rio, Venice, Vienna) series.

OAKLEAF HYDRANGEAS

'Little Honey'; 'Pee Wee'; 'Ruby Slippers'; 'Munchkin'; and 'Sikes Dwarf'.

PANICULATAS

'Bombshell'; 'Dharuma'; 'Kyushu'; Little Lime™; 'Pee Wee'; and White Diamonds™.

Hydrangeas purchased for indoor use can be planted in the garden later. They will not bloom again until the following season.

Forced Hydrangeas

Potted hydrangeas with giant flower heads are popular gifts on Easter and Mother's Day. Hydrangeas normally bloom mid- to late summer. These florist hydrangeas are forced into bloom much sooner than normal, and they are allowed just a few flower heads so that the flowers will be larger than normal for that big impact so important in the commercial trade. As a result of all this manipulation the plants are weaker than those grown to be sold at garden centers and are less likely to thrive in the garden. That said, this doesn't mean they can't thrive in the garden, just that their chances are not as good as those bred for the outdoors.

If you throw away a plant it has no chance for success; if you plant it, it has some chance. Many people have good luck planting forced hydrangeas in the garden, including the author who has heard from many others reporting similar successes. You have nothing to lose if you try, and a beautiful garden plant to gain if you succeed.

It is quite possible that the variety called 'Penny Mac', named for Penny McHenry, the founder of the American Hydrangea Society, was originally a forced plant. She was given a hydrangea as a gift and propagated it widely. Later it was found to be particularly hardy.

A closeup of one of the twenty-five cent hydrangeas in the garden. The author is happy to have rescued such a beautiful plant.

When the neglected hydrangeas were purchased for twenty-five cents, the flowers had all gone by. One of the joys of rescuing such plants is seeing the different flowers as they emerge the following year. All were different and all, including this lovely lacecap, were beautiful in their own way.

These hydrangeas were purchased for twenty-five cents apiece at a garden center in late April. The remnants of that season's Easter plants, they had been neglected for a few weeks. With just a little basic nurturing (fresh garden soil, old flowers snipped off, fertilizer and water applied), they resumed healthy growth and were planted in the author's garden in the fall, where they grow larger and more beautiful every year.

If you do decide to plant a forced hydrangea in the garden, it is a good idea to check the roots. They may have become cramped in the pot. Sometimes a lack of available space in the pot causes the roots to circle around. If this is the case, you will need to tease the roots apart and loosen them so they have a fighting chance of taking hold and spreading out in the garden.

Please note, these forced plants are often on the small side and should be planted at the front of a flower bed.

HOW TO PLAN FOR SEASONAL ADJUSTMENTS

12

Understanding Normal Bloom Time and Color Changes

I magine you are visiting Nantucket and, on a pleasant walk around your B&B, you see a lovely display of hydrangeas with big round blue flowers side by side with big round white flowers. Where they are closest together the flowers have intermixed. Because you love blue and white together, this is a combination that appeals to you completely. On your next trip to Nantucket you remember that beautiful display and take your friend who also loves the blue and white combination to see it too. But something is wrong. The plants must have been moved and other plants put in their place. Instead of blue and white flowers you see green and burgundy flowers. What happened?

An early July view in the author's back yard. The flowers of the mophead in the foreground appear in many different colors which is not unusual in the early stages of development.

What happened is that the flowers matured into their antique colors. Some blue mopheads take on burgundy tones in the fall. The big snowball-like white flowers of *Hydrangea arborescens*

In mid-July the flowers have settled into their typical solid blue color.

'Annabelle' first emerge green in the spring and change back to green as summer ends. This is a natural progression; the blue and white flowers of summer become the burgundy and green flowers of autumn.

The same shrub in early October. The flowers have turned a rich shade of burgundy (they will dry in that color) and they have a more ruffled appearance as some of the sepals have turned upside down.

Not all blue mopheads change to a burgundy color in the fall. This one ages to a lovely shade of light purple. The photo was taken in early August.

The formerly blue mophead has aged to light purple. Photo taken in early October.

Blue mopheads draw the eye in early July on Cape Cod.

Bloom time

Most hydrangea flowers go through similar color changes. Some gardeners extend the prime bloom season of mopheads by planting some varieties that bloom early, some in mid-season, and some that bloom late. The varieties known to be rebloomers will bloom again later in the season if the first flowers are removed. (See Chapter 7 for a list of rebloomers.)

Mopheads. Early flowering mopheads include 'Freudenstein', 'Frillibet', 'Gerda Steiniger', 'Nikko Blue', and 'Renate Steiniger'.

Late flowering mopheads include 'Amethyst', 'Ayesha', 'Blauer Prinz', 'King George', and 'Niedersachsen'.

Blue lacecaps, early August, Cape Cod.

By early October the formerly blue lacecaps have aged to a faded pink shade.

Lacecaps. The flowers of lacecap varieties also change color as the season progresses. The outer sepals turn dramatically upside down by the end of the season. Two varieties known to produce late flowers are 'Lanarth White' and 'Kardinal'.

The sepals of lacecaps characteristically turn upside down as the flowers age.

By mid-August the blue mopheads have faded to their antique colors. Notice the purple hydrangeas on the shrub at the right. These flowers appeared later than the blue flowers. Hydrangea shrubs can be early-, mid-, or late-blooming.

An oakleaf hydrangea with white summer blooms in July on Cape Cod.

At some point later in the season the white oakleaf flowers of summer start going through autumn color changes. This photo, taken in late August, shows the flowers in an early pink stage. The pink color deepens as the season progresses.

Eventually oakleaf flowers turn chocolate brown, while the foliage takes on rich fall colors.

Oakleaf hydrangeas. The flowers of the oakleaf hydrangeas progress seasonally from white flowers during the heat of the summer to various stages of pink and ultimately to a rich chocolate brown. Many oakleaf varieties are also known for beautiful fall foliage.

Climbing hydrangeas. The flowers of climbing hydrangeas merely fade away, but the foliage in the fall changes dramatically. *Hydrangea petiolaris* has foliage in a rich dark green through most of the summer, but in the fall it turns a glorious golden yellow. It is a background player in the summer but in the spring it is notable for its flowers and in the fall it makes another important presence with its foliage.

Climbing hydrangea foliage provides a green background for summer flowers in the garden.

The foliage of a climbing hydrangea in the fall turns a glorious golden yellow.

The flowers of *Hydrangea arborescens* 'Annabelle' are green when they first emerge, then white for many weeks before they revert to green in the fall.

The emerging flowers of *Hydrangea arborescens* 'Hayes Starburst' on July 3rd on Cape Cod.

Ten days later, July 13th, 'Hayes Starburst' is clearly headed toward its full summer white.

By July 29th, 'Hayes Starburst' has attained fully developed white blooms.

'Hayes Starburst' at left ages to green. This photo was taken on August 21st next to the white flowers of H.p. 'Limelight'.

Arborescens varieties. The flowers of *Hydrangea arborescens* are usually green in the spring, white in the summer, and green again in the fall. It is not unusual to see a mix of green and white flowers in late spring when they are heading toward their summer season color.

Paniculatas. The panicle hydrangeas are the latest to bloom, usually coming into their own when the mopheads are starting to fade. Many paniculata varieties have white (or cream) flowers in their prime and then progress through various shades of pink and burgundy. The distinctive variety called 'Limelight' is known for its green flower color before turning white.

In late August at Heritage Gardens in Sandwich, Massachusetts, the flowers of *Hydrangea paniculata* 'Limelight' are completely white.

One month later the flowers of H.p. 'Limelight' are progressing through fall color changes.

It is not unusual for a single paniculata shrub to show blooms in different colors at the same time. Flowers in full sun will bloom sooner than those in the shade.

A very young flower of *Hydrangea paniculata* Pink Diamond™ with its white color apparently contradicting its name. This photo was taken in early July on Cape Cod.

H.p. Pink Diamond™ on September 25th when it has become the pink color indicated in its name. The deep pink shade is attained after it starts white then turns a paler pink before deepening to its ultimate color.

Planning for seasonal adjustment

Review the color change information above when selecting hydrangeas for your garden. Understanding the normal progression of color should help you make good decisions about which hydrangeas will work well for you.

HOW AND WHEN TO PRUNE HYDRANGEAS

13

Keeping Plants in Good Shape

*H*ow should I prune my hydrangeas? When should I prune them? These are the most common pruning questions, but another important question often overlooked by gardeners new to hydrangeas is: *Should I prune my hydrangeas at all?* The good news is that many hydrangeas require very little pruning. They will produce quite satisfactory results if left to their own devices. Before discussing techniques and timing (the how and when of pruning) here are some guidelines to help you decide whether you need to prune at all.

Reasons for Pruning

Damage control. Broken stems are unsightly and offer openings for pests and diseases to enter the plant. Damage can occur as the result of acts of nature (heavy snow and/or ice in winter, hail, and severe wind at any time of year) and acts of careless humans and pets.

Early spring is a good time to check your plants for signs of damage, or any time the area has sustained a lot of human or animal traffic. Broken stems should be cut back or off completely depending on the extent of the damage.

Keep in mind that plants can be resilient. It is not a bad idea to wait for a few days to see if part or all of the plant will bounce back after injury. The author was once dismayed to see a favorite lacecap shrub flattened completely after a severe winter. After about a week of spring warmth the entire center portion of the shrub recovered. By then it was clear what would survive and what needed attention.

Damage control includes anticipating future damage, as when branches are crossed and rubbing against each other. The friction will inevitably weaken one or more affected branches. Select the best one to save and remove the other(s). Choosing the best branch is a matter of judgment having to do with relative sturdiness and its contribution to the appearance of the shrub as a whole.

Disease control. Fortunately hydrangeas are not prone to many diseases. Powdery mildew is usually the worst you will have to contend with. As with any plant, the healthier the plant the more it will be able to resist pests and diseases. If you notice worrisome symptoms like holes in the leaves or leaf discoloration your first tendency might be to remove the offending leaves or entire branches from the shrub. This may be an overreaction. First try to determine what is causing the problem since how you deal with the problem depends on its cause. Is it a disease problem or a pest problem? For example, you might think your mophead is diseased when you notice once-healthy leaves seem to be breaking apart irregularly around the edges. What is more likely is that slugs found your shrub and are happily nibbling away at it. This is particularly likely if it is the succulent new growth that is affected. Control for slugs and eliminate the problem. Once the slugs are gone you can remove unsightly leaves (or parts of leaves) to improve the overall appearance of the shrub.

When symptoms develop and you don't know the cause, check with your local university extension service which often provides hotlines staffed by master gardeners. Their primary goal is to help you, the home gardener, do the right thing for your plants. Be prepared to

Spots like this that are tan in the middle portion with purple around the edges alert you to a fungal problem often caused by overhead watering. Remove the affected leaves.

Leaf damage can be caused by pests. Here the pest in question is visible in the bottom of the v-shaped damage in the upper leaf. Remove pests by hand when you spot them; seek advice from master gardeners when you can't see what critter is causing the damage.

The author went to brush a pine needle off this leaf. It didn't brush off easily because it was impaled in the leaf. Tugging it out of the leaf caused this hole. Sometimes damage to leaves is due to twigs, branches, and pine needles falling from above.

describe the affected area as clearly as possible and include any possible relevant information, especially recent changes in that section of the garden.

Many leaf spots are fungal in nature. One called *cercospora hydrangeae* is most noticeable in the fall with symptomatic tan lesions with dark purple halos. Late summer rain can make the problem more severe. As with any fungal infection, it is important to keep the area clean. Pluck off diseased leaves and don't put them in the compost pile; get rid of them. When the plant loses all leaves in late fall, rake them up and dispose of them. When new leaves appear the following spring keep an eye on the plant for recurring symptoms and treat with a fungicide. If in doubt about whether what you are looking at is a fungus, bring the affected foliage to your university extension agent or to your local garden center for advice.

Overall appearance. What you want is a pleasing appearance in which nothing jarring catches the eye. Stand back from a shrub and let your eyes wander over it. Is there anything that bothers you? Perhaps a stem is elevated much higher than its neighbors. A skinny weak stem might be too close to the ground, detracting from the otherwise vase shape of the plant. A vigorous side branch could be partially blocking a walking path in the garden as well as being unsightly. Any such element is a candidate for removal. Detailed pruning advice can be found later in the chapter but for now just think about how to evaluate the appearance of your shrub.

You also want to consider the appearance of the flowers. At the end of the season the flowers go through various changes. Some change color, some get scorched around the edges from sun that is too intense, and all fade to some extent as they begin the process of drying. Before removing them you should keep the following questions in mind.

- *Do I want to dry some flowers later in the season?*

If this is the case, remove only those you don't care to save for harvest.

- *Do I live in a climate where winter protection is important?*

In harsher climates it is a good idea to wait until spring to remove spent flowers since they provide an extra layer of cover to the shrub.

- *How important is the winter appearance of the shrub?*

If your hydrangea is highly visible during the winter months and the look of dead flowers would bother you, remove them.

Caution: Protect your eyes when pruning hydrangeas. Sharp sticks can be hiding right under new leaves.

The shrub with the blue flowers on the bottom was pruned at the wrong time of year. The top of the shrub was pruned back in the fall, probably to clear the view from the window. In the spring the shrub grew to the size it wanted to be, but without flowers on the top portion. The flower buds were removed the previous fall. To ensure flowers all over your shrubs, prune in the summer immediately after flowering, or wait until the following spring to prune *lightly*.

Here is a mophead shrub in early spring with new foliage interspersed with brown sticks which should be removed.

There is no need for drastic pruning. The plant should just look tidied up as a result of the pruning, not severely cut back. This photo shows the plant one week later than the previous picture after light pruning has been done.

Controlling plant size. We try our best to put the right plant in the right place but size problems can develop nonetheless. A common problem is the shrub that has grown too tall or has spread too wide for its space in the garden. Now what? It is a natural tendency to cut it back, but by doing so you might be reinvigorating the plant, provoking a growth spurt, the opposite of what you want. Or you might cut it back at the wrong time of year resulting in the loss of flowers for the following growing season. You need to understand how your particular hydrangea(s) will respond to pruning activities.

A better solution to fighting a plant that keeps trying to be the size it wants to be is to move it to a location where its size is appropriate and replace it with a smaller variety. If this is impractical, you could try a selective approach. Rather than cutting all the stems back drastically, cut only half of them in the spring, interspersed throughout the shrub. Cut the other half just to the first leaf node. This way you will have flowers from the buds set the previous fall on the stems you have only lightly trimmed. In the fall cut the stems with flowers back drastically. It may take a few years to get this shrub back into control and keep this in mind: if you have a variety that wants to be five feet tall, it is going to keep working to get there.

When and How to Prune

The timing of pruning depends on the species. Details are provided below on when to prune the different species and how to go about it. Keep in mind that it is better not to prune at all than to prune incorrectly or at the wrong time of year. When in doubt, leave the plant alone!

Hydrangea macrophylla (mopheads and lacecaps)

Flowering shrubs in general should be pruned immediately after flowering, before the buds are set for the following year's blooms. If you choose to leave this year's flowers on the shrub until later in

The same plant in full bloom in mid-summer.

When in doubt cut into a stem near the top of the plant to see if it is still alive. These two stems looked about the same from the outside. The stem on the left is green inside indicating it was still alive when cut. The stem on the right is clearly dead.

the season because you want to harvest them for drying, this is not a problem. Next year's flower buds will appear on the flowerless straight shoots you see now. Those are the ones that will branch out and flower the following season.

There is no absolute need to do any pruning during the summer. You can leave the shrub alone and wait until spring. If you do prune in the summer, prune only the stems that carried flowers. The new straight flowerless shoots without side branches will eventually branch out and produce the next year's flowers so leave them alone. **Avoid pruning mopheads and lacecaps in the fall as you may be removing all the buds for next year's flowers.**

Spring is a good time to assess this species when new growth appears. Young hydrangeas (those planted in your garden within the last three years) should be pruned only lightly. Remove old flowers and the brown twigs near the top of the stems, cutting back to where you see the fresh green growth. Remove dead stems completely. Your goal should be merely to tidy up the plant, not to make drastic cuts.

Older shrubs might require more drastic pruning. If a shrub is over five years old some of the stems will have grown large in diameter, crowding the plant at the base. To rejuvenate the plant and increase air circulation it is a good idea to remove about a third of the old stems every year, right down to the ground, even if they are showing healthy new buds. This will stimulate the growth of newer stems and keep the plant vigorous. In the spring after

you have removed all the obviously dead stems, study the base of the plant. Find the fattest stems. Let's say there are nine of them. You should remove three of them, evenly spaced around the plant for the sake of balance. Once a year do the same thing for mature plants; remove about a third of the oldest stems.

Usually it is obvious when a stem has died but if you have any doubt at all make a cut near the top of the stem. A dead stem shows no green color inside. If you see green inside the stem, it is still alive.

Still more drastic action might be required for plants that have been seriously neglected for years. If you feel overwhelmed by the time and effort required to deal with such plants you can save yourself a lot of work by simply cutting them down to about knee-high. Please note, you will likely sacrifice a year's worth of blooms if you choose to go this route, but it might be the most practical approach. People who have done this have reported plants back to five or six feet high within two years.

Hydrangea paniculata (panicle hydrangeas)

Paniculatas, like the popular Pee Gee, bloom on new wood. What that means is they bloom on the current season's growth. If you prune them in the fall you don't have to worry that you will lose flowers the following year as

In early spring these paniculata shrubs at Heritage Gardens in Sandwich, Massachusetts, have been significantly cut back.

The same shrubs in late August of the same year. The variety is H.p. 'Limelight'.

you would with the mopheads and lacecaps. If you live in an area where a spring thaw can be followed by a severe freeze you don't have to worry about vulnerable new buds being damaged. In fact, you can cut a paniculata back severely in late winter or early spring and it will grow long stems and produce gorgeous flowers that same year.

Whether or not to prune paniculatas depends on the end result you are aiming for. If you want a bushy shrub with a lot of smaller flowers, you need to do very little pruning, limiting it to general cleanup. If you want a neat, more erect shrub with larger flowers, you need to prune. With pruning you have fewer flowers but the flowers will be larger than

they would have been had you not pruned at all. To summarize: **If you prune paniculatas you will have larger flowers but they will be fewer in number than if you didn't prune at all. If you don't prune you will have plenty of smaller flowers on a bushier shrub**.

If you decide to prune you should do it in the late winter or early spring before new growth starts. Prune back the main stems

to about one-half inch above the lower set of buds. Paniculatas usually have three buds at each level; each of the main stems will result in three branches and, therefore, three blossoms. For cultivars with heavy blooms (like 'Grandiflora', 'Limelight', and 'Phantom'), aim for at least ten main stems to support the weight of the blooms.

Hydrangea arborescens (smooth leaf hydrangeas like 'Annabelle')

Similar to the paniculatas this species can be cut down in the spring before new growth appears to about twelve to eighteen inches high. You will not be losing any potential flowers because they bloom on new wood, i.e. the current season's wood. New stems will grow quickly so don't worry about cutting them down this drastically.

Hydrangea quercifolia (oakleaf hydrangeas)

The oakleaf hydrangea blooms on old wood, like the macrophyllas, so prune these plants lightly in the spring when new growth appears. This species generally requires very little pruning. What you should concentrate on is removing dead wood and any crossed branches that might weaken the shrub.

Hydrangea petiolaris (climbing hydrangea)

Climbing hydrangeas need very little pruning. Keep an eye on growth at ground level that might show an inclination to roam to a new territory. Otherwise its location will determine whether you need to prune it. Side shoots on a trellis, for instance, might encroach on a narrow garden path. If it is climbing on a garden shed or house you might have to cut around a window or door.

Pruning is both art and science. Once you understand the basics of pruning each species you can concentrate more on pruning as an art form. The aesthetic goal is to make each shrub as visually pleasing as possible during the growing season.

You can prune out bare sticks at any time during the growing season but it is much easier to do in early spring before lush foliage and large flowers get in the way.

HOW TO PROPAGATE HYDRANGEAS

14

Creating New Plants

There are three methods commonly used to propagate hydrangeas: taking cuttings; layering; and dividing existing plants. The method you choose will depend on the situation. Once you understand your options it should be obvious which method to use in a given situation.

Who wouldn't want a cutting of this lovely lacecap?

Taking Cuttings

Consider these situations:

- You have always admired the magnificent lacecap hydrangea in your neighbor's yard, the one you can see from your kitchen window every day. You have been meaning to ask for a cutting but haven't gotten around to it yet. Now you have learned your neighbor is planning to sell the house and you worry the new owners will remove that wonderful hydrangea. You know you have to act…now!

- You fall in love with a deep blue mophead in your friend's garden. Your friend doesn't know the name of the plant and you can't seem to find that same gorgeous deep blue color on any hydrangea offered for sale at local garden centers. One sure way of getting the same plant for your own garden is to take a cutting.

- You have amassed a wonderful collection of hydrangeas but now you are planning to move to another state. The simplest way to take your collection with you is in the form of cuttings.

These kinds of situations are what usually prompt hydrangea lovers to learn how to take cuttings if they don't know how already. The principles apply to a wide variety of plant materials so the benefits of this knowledge are substantial.

Cloning your plants. Propagating your plants by taking cuttings is essentially cloning. The resulting baby plants are identical to the parent plant in all essential characteristics. If the parent plant has sturdy stems or deep blue flowers or a wonderful vase-like form, the baby plant will too. Take care to select the healthiest plant possible from which to take cuttings.

Taking cuttings is easy. Don't be intimidated by this if you have never done it before. If you follow the simple guidelines detailed in this chapter you are likely to have success. Hydrangeas, bless them, seem eager to reproduce themselves so even if you fumble around a bit at first, there's still a good chance the cuttings will root. Once you have mastered the technique you can go on to take cuttings of a wide variety of plants, which leads to the next point.

Taking cuttings is inexpensive. Think about the cost of loading up your cart at the local garden center. It is often a shock to learn how much it adds up to but still, you *want* all these plants! On the other hand, all you need to clone existing plants are pots, some fresh potting soil, cutting tools, and rooting hormone (if you have it but it is not absolutely essential), all materials you may already have in your potting area.

Taking cuttings takes little time. In well under an hour you can take a dozen or more hydrangea cuttings and process them completely, from snipping them off the shrubs to potting them up, ready to settle in to whatever location you have chosen where they may sit undisturbed while they develop nice healthy roots. Once you learn the basics, the processing time can be much shorter, if mass production is what you are after. The point is it takes very little time to create baby hydrangeas.

Taking cuttings is satisfying. There is something particularly gratifying in looking at a magnificent plant in your garden that started life as a cutting you took from another plant. It is like looking at your children and remembering them as babies.

Sharing with friends is a generous thing to do. Hydrangeas are very popular at plant swap gatherings.

The growth rate of hydrangeas is remarkable. A tiny cutting in a four-inch pot can become a substantial garden plant in only three years.

Prepare the Pots

Four-inch plastic pots work well. Plastic is preferable to clay because it retains moisture better. If you are reusing plastic pots make sure they have been cleaned well. Fill the desired number of pots about three-quarters full with a nice light potting soil. Do not use garden soil. A good quality bagged potting soil contains nutrients and has the right texture for good growing conditions. Garden soil is often too heavy and dense. This is also the case with many lower grade packaged potting soils. A heavy dense soil will lead to poor drainage and root rot. Water the soil and allow it to drain for several minutes before inserting cuttings. You want the soil moist but not soaking wet.

Alternatively you could fill the pots with such rooting media as vermiculite, perlite, and sand (but not sand from the beach which would be too salty). These are excellent because they are sterile and promote good drainage. The disadvantage is the lack of nutrients; once roots form the cuttings have to be repotted using potting soil. The author has had good luck rooting hydrangeas in potting soil thus eliminating an extra step.

The clean pots are ready for potting soil. Each 4" pot can hold 4 cuttings. The six trays of twelve pots each can hold a grand total of 288 cuttings. Notice how little space this takes up.

The pots with potting soil added have been watered and are draining before cuttings are inserted.

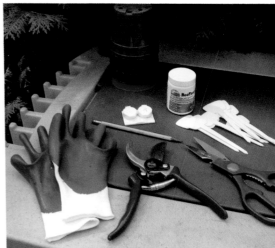

Materials needed for taking cuttings. The old contact lens case is used for small amounts of the rooting hormone.

Materials Needed to Take Cuttings

You will need plastic pots, a potting medium (potting soil or vermiculite, perlite, or sterile sand), pruners, scissors, rooting hormone (recommended but not required), dibber (a pencil with an eraser end works fine), plant labels, and permanent marker.

Take Cuttings from the Parent Plant

The best time of year to take cuttings is in spring when growth is vigorous, but cuttings can be taken any time during the growing season. The later in the season you do this, the longer it will take for the cuttings to root.

Look for plant tips without flowers. These can be found on the top of the plant or along the sides. Fresh new growth is preferable to older growth. You can tell the relative age by the distance between the nodes. (The nodes are swellings along the stem, usually marked by the presence of leaves.) The closer the nodes, the younger the stem. A good size for cuttings is about six inches. The cuttings start losing moisture quickly so it is best to work with just a few at a time. (If you want to take many cuttings on one day and pot them up later, wrap their stems in a damp paper towel, put them in a plastic bag, and put the bag in the refrigerator for up to a few days.)

Step-by-step Procedure for Potting Up Your Cuttings

- At the top of the cutting pinch out any growth between the top two leaves. This is where a flower bud would form. You want all the energy to go downward to the roots instead of to the development of a flower bud.

- Working from the bottom of the cutting rip off all leaves (most will snap off easily) except the top two leaves. With scissors cut the top two leaves in half. The reason for this is to reduce the cutting's need for water.

Try to find cuttings where the nodes are close together. This is young new growth, the best for cuttings.

Cuttings dry out quickly so take just a few at a time and get them potted up before cutting more.

The bottom of a cutting with just a light dusting of rooting hormone.

99

- With pruners, make an angle cut below the bottom node.

- Dip the end in rooting hormone. Don't be concerned if you don't have any rooting hormone. Some plants require rooting hormone for propagation success but hydrangeas are not quite so fussy. The use of rooting hormone does speed the rate of rooting and often increases the number of roots so if you have it, by all means, use it.

    You should avoid dipping cuttings in large containers of rooting hormone, to prevent contamination should the cutting be diseased. Transfer small amounts to a separate container like a jar lid. The author uses an old contact lens case which can be shut quickly when rain or wind make work conditions less than favorable. Tap off any excess rooting hormone. Too much can be toxic. Aim for a light coating. It should look like a dusting of powder.

- You can fit three or four cuttings in one four-inch pot. Use a dibber or the eraser end of a pencil to make a hole in the soil, taking care not to go to the very bottom of the pot. You want the bottom of the cutting in soil, not resting against the pot. The reason for making this hole is for the rooting hormone to stay at the bottom of the

cutting when it is placed in the soil. Insert the cutting in the hole and slightly firm the soil around it. Once all the cuttings have been placed in that pot add more soil, firm it around the cuttings, water again, and drain once more. Insert a label to show which variety you have in the pot. If you don't know the name of the variety, at least indicate the source. It might say something like "Barbara's purple lacecap" or "Diane's mother's mophead".

- Place the pots in a shady, wind-protected location, like under a shrub in a sheltered area in your yard. Keep the soil moist, but not too wet. Roots can form in as little as two weeks. Once the cuttings have formed a good root system, transfer each cutting into a pot of its own in a good quality potting soil.

Layering

Layering is one of nature's ways of self-propagation. When a stem near the base of a plant touches the ground it sometimes roots in place. Eventually this grows up to be another plant. Oftentimes masses of plants in wild settings originated with a single plant. You can choose to propagate this way, especially if you spot a stem hovering close to the ground. This method can be used for propagation in the

When using the layering method, push the stem down to the ground to see where it will naturally rest on the ground.

Anchor the layered stem with something heavy like a rock or a brick.

spring or the summer and it is also a good activity for fall as part of the annual garden cleanup. Make a point of walking around your garden looking to see where you might do some layering. If you choose to propagate by layering you would be in good company. Penny McHenry, the founder of the American Hydrangea Society, did this all the time, eventually turning her two hydrangeas into more than four hundred plants.

Once you find a good candidate, press on the branch to see where part of it would naturally touch the soil if weight were applied to it. Loosen the soil here, digging a small trough. Slightly wound the underside of the stem where it will meet the soil. You can either cut a small slit in the underside of the stem with a sharp knife or just scrape it with a fingernail. Strip off the leaves in the immediate area. Press the branch down to meet the prepared hole, cover that section of the branch with fresh soil, and weight the branch securely. A brick or large rock will do this job nicely. Once the steps are completed you play a waiting game. You will want to keep the soil in that area well watered but other than that your job is done; the rest is up to the plant. Allow about a year to pass before tugging gently on the layered section to see if it has rooted. (Usually you can tell it has if you see fresh growth in that area.) Once it has rooted, cut it from the parent plant. Leave it in place for a month or so before moving it to a new location. This gives it a good chance to survive and thrive on its own. (You don't have to move it at all. Some gardeners use this technique to create lovely sweeps of the same plant.)

The layering method is easy, costs practically nothing, takes little time, and no special equipment is needed. The offspring will be identical to the parent plant. If you don't mind what it looks like, and depending on the space available, one plant can be layered in several directions at the same time.

Dividing

This method calls for a plant to be separated into two or more segments each with its own root system. Dig up the plant and divide with a sharp spade. Plant the segments, either in containers or in the garden, and cut stems back to about half their original length. This is a good method when you wish you had two of that plant instead of one.

Some plants need to be divided every few years to maintain good health and vigor. Hydrangeas are not in this group; they do not need to be divided to thrive. If the shrubs are happy in their location they can be left alone to grow into their ultimate mature size. There are times, though, when division should be considered.

You might have an unidentified hydrangea variety in your garden that you love. You would like to plant one just like it in another spot in your garden but, since you don't know the name of the variety, you can't just go to a garden center and purchase another one. You could take cuttings of the plant in question but then you would have to wait about three years for it to reach the size you want it to be now. Division is the logical solution.

Another obvious call for division occurs when a hydrangea is tangled up with another plant and the two plants need to be separated. Dig them both up, tease the roots apart, and, before replanting the hydrangea, see if you can divide it easily to create more than one plant.

Sometimes when a hydrangea is being transplanted, it falls into two or more segments on its own, in which case it has very kindly divided itself, sparing the gardener's time and effort. Each segment may be planted on its own, as long as it has a good root system.

Spring and fall are both good times of the year for successful division of hydrangeas, since the air tends to be cooler than during the summer months and the plants are less likely to suffer transplant shock. For the same reason plan to divide plants in the morning or evening on the day you have selected. Try for a calm day since wind tends to dry a plant out quickly, and allow yourself enough time to dig up the plant, divide it, replant all the resulting segments, and water them in thoroughly.

Note: late fall is the best possible time because they then have time to settle into their new locations before having to deal with the stress of heat.

Arborescens varieties are easy to divide because they can be drastically pruned back in the winter and they bloom on new wood. Dig up the root ball, slice it into quarters, and replant the pieces.

Knowing these three propagation methods allows you to decide how to propagate your hydrangeas and gives you the satisfaction of increasing your collection without heading off to the garden center. If you teach your hydrangea loving friends to do the same you can have a productive plant swap party; a win-win situation for everyone.

A climbing hydrangea planted at the base of a tree supporting a hammock started creeping away from the tree. This section was separated from the parent plant and carried over to the base of the other tree where it then began climbing in its new location. Result: two climbing hydrangeas for the price of one.

HOW TO PREPARE FRESH FLOWER ARRANGEMENTS

15

Cutting Stems for Indoor Enjoyment

The very first hydrangea blooms have appeared on your hydrangea shrubs early in the season. You are delighted, as always, with their loveliness and decide to cut some so you can enjoy them inside the house as well. Perhaps you have guests coming for dinner and you picture a gorgeous lush centerpiece. The arrangement ends up looking as wonderful as you imagined, but by the time your guests sit down to dinner it is looking sad and droopy, the flowers already wilting. What did you do wrong?

A lot of yellow in the flower means it is not fully developed. The one on the left is too new to be picked for a floral arrangement.

This flower is close to being fully developed but is not quite ready to be picked for an arrangement.

Timing Is Everything

You picked the flowers too soon. As with many things in life, timing is crucial. The flower needs to be fully developed before you cut it to display indoors. What does "fully developed" mean? It means the flower has had time to open fully on the shrub and has completely attained its mature color. You want the flower to be completely blue (or pink or purple or white) before cutting it for use indoors. This process usually takes at least a week. The older the bloom, the longer the cut flower will last in water.

This requirement guarantees frustration for those who love newly emerging blossoms more than any other; the ones with the soft colors mixed with shades of green or yellow. These blooms cannot last long as cut flowers. To avoid constant disappointment, people who love these early flowers should resign themselves to appreciating them outside on the flowering shrubs.

When all conditions are right, fresh cut hydrangeas should last for a week and sometimes two weeks. If hydrangeas as cut flowers are important to you it is a good idea to plant varieties in your garden that are known to produce good cut flowers.

Cut in the Morning

Early morning is the best time to cut hydrangeas for fresh arrangements because at that time of day they are full of water. If you can't cut them in the morning, a second-best time is in the late afternoon or evening. It is important to avoid cutting them in the heat of the day. Have a container of water handy because water loss occurs as soon as you cut them. Advice on water temperature is conflicting. Cool, lukewarm, very warm, all have been recommended by florists, cut flower specialists, and a variety of horticulturists. Not debated is the need for water, immediately, as soon as the flower is cut. Cut them slightly longer than needed

Cut flowers with fully developed color.

so you can recut them just before adding them to the arrangement. With your pruners cut the stem at an angle to allow it to take in water easily and to prevent the kind of blockage that occurs when a stem cut straight across rests flat against the bottom of the container. Then use sharp scissors to make a vertical cut of about two inches at the base of the stem. This second cut will further help the stem take up water. Remove most or all of the leaves immediately, before placing the stem in water. The big leaves require a lot of water and you want the water going to the flowers so they will look their best. If you love the look of the leaves with the flowers, cut a few stems with just leaves to add to your arrangement.

Conditioning

While it is possible to add the flowers to an arrangement as soon as you bring them indoors, you will have flowers that look better and last longer if you condition them first. Conditioning is designed to counteract the inevitable slight wilting that occurs when the flowers are removed from the shrub. You want the flowers filled with water again when you create your arrangement. Allow a few hours for conditioning.

Submerge the flowers. Ideally you would submerge the flowers, stems and all, for at least an hour. This is not always practical, especially if you don't have a

container large enough for this purpose. A bathtub works but it might be inconvenient for the family to have it filled with flowers. Second best is to submerge the flower heads, either in a container or in a deep sink, for about twenty minutes before going on to the next step.

Place stems in water. Have handy the container in which you will condition the flowers. A tall kitchen wastebasket works well. As it will be heavy when filled with water and flowers, it is a good idea to place it where the conditioning will occur before you get started. Fill with enough water so that the water will cover half the stem length and add a **floral preservative**. Adding a floral preservative will help keep cut flowers fresh for a longer period of time. Most commercial floral preservatives are a mix of ingredients designed to address the specific needs of cut flowers: **sugar** to supply nutrients; **acid** to prevent bacterial growth and to help the plant take in water and food; and a **disinfectant** to reduce the possibility of disease which would lead to premature decay. If you don't have any commercial floral preservative available, you can follow a home recipe such as the following: 1 teaspoon sugar + 2 teaspoons lemon juice added to 1 quart of lukewarm water. Stir and add 1 teaspoon of bleach.

Submerging the flowerheads helps to fill them with water, with the added advantage of provoking any lurking insects to scurry up the side of the container, away from the flowers.

This tall kitchen wastebasket was placed on cool tile in an air conditioned bathroom away from the direct light from a window; a good place for conditioning the flowers before placing them in flower arrangements.

Place the stems in the water to which the floral preservative has been added and add more water. To keep the flower heads well hydrated, cover them with white (no dye) dampened paper towels. Put the container in a cool area for several hours.

Arrange the Flowers

Once the flowers have been conditioned, have on hand a clean container filled with water to which floral preservative has been added. **Note: the shorter the stems needed (as in a short vase or bowl), the longer the life of the cut flowers.** The flower arrangement will last longer and look as fresh as possible if protected from sources of heat and draft which would dry it out and make the flower color fade.

Check the Water Regularly

Add water as needed and change the water completely every few days. When you change the water it is a good idea to recut the stems.

Containers

Vases, bowls, watering cans, baskets, glasses, and mugs can look wonderful when filled with just the right hydrangeas to suit them. Sometimes simple arrangements are the most striking, like a big white pitcher filled with white 'Limelight' hydrangeas, a short stainless steel ice cream dish with one blue mophead, or a footed milk glass bowl filled with deep purple mopheads with glossy hydrangea leaves all along the sides of the bowl.

Flowers with short stems last longer than those with long stems.

A wide glass vase holds the flowers inside this appropriately decorated metal container. *Decorative painting on container by Elaine Wright.*

A watering can with a floral motif seemed perfect for these soft blue hydrangeas.

White containers are perfect for any color hydrangea. Here pink mopheads and lacecaps are combined into a unified color scheme.

A margarita glass set inside the metal container adds a second tier to the floral design.

A simple and lovely arrangement in a white ceramic basket. *Arrangement by Mary Kay Condon.*

A coffee mug sets a nautical theme at a Cape Cod party.

A glass vase for the flowers was set inside this Nantucket basket before the arrangement was made.

One blue mophead filled this cobalt blue bottle found while traveling in Belgium.

If you plant many different varieties of hydrangeas in your garden, you increase the options when creating flower arrangements.

roses and the chartreuse flowers of lady's mantle. White mopheads can be teamed with the white-edged leaves of the hosta variety called 'Patriot'. Blue mopheads with yellow calla lilies make a vibrant arrangement.

Take advantage of what your garden has to offer on a given day. Cut one small hydrangea stem and carry it around the garden, holding it up next to anything blooming at the same time. Note which

The containers should be able to support the hydrangeas without the use of floral foam which seems to shorten the life of cut hydrangeas. If the container you are working with has a wide opening, like a tureen or punch bowl, you might consider using chicken wire as an aid to create support, or crisscross a grid across the top with floral tape.

Floral companions

Hydrangeas alone make a powerful impact but you might also want to combine them with other flowers from the garden. Mopheads in a medium pink shade look wonderful with deep pink

White lacecap blossoms provide starry accents to an arrangement of blue and purple mopheads.

flowers go particularly well with the hydrangea. Don't forget to check it against the foliage of various plants as well, including annuals, perennials, shrubs, and ground covers. Once you see what works well, go ahead and cut what you will need for indoor arrangements. The more you do this, the more fun you will have filling your favorite containers with beautiful hydrangeas from your garden.

A vibrant arrangement featuring blue and white mopheads with companion flowers.

This arrangement of a blue mophead with a white paniculata and a pink dahlia was made to decorate a table at a picnic in mid-August on Cape Cod. *Arrangement by Kathy Bakanas.*

Pink hydrangeas and roses in a bride's bouquet. *Floral design by Katie McConnell, Wild Bunch Studio, Chatham, Massachusetts.*

An exuberant arrangement of white, blue, pink, and purple hydrangeas, a prize winner in a Cape Cod Hydrangea Society flower arranging contest. *Arrangement by Joan Brazeau.*

Tangerine tulips are combined with white hydrangeas in this stunning wedding centerpiece. *Floral design by R Blooms, Lake Oswego, Oregon.*

Several mophead varieties combined beautifully. *Arrangement by Deborah McCauley-Buck, Moonshell Design, Chatham, Massachusetts.*

A patriotic arrangement at Heritage Gardens in Sandwich, Massachusetts, featuring white paniculatas with red roses in a blue vase.

Hydrangea Varieties Known to Produce Good Cut Flowers

'Altona'; 'Blushing Pink'; 'Böttstein'; 'Bouquet Rose'; 'Deutschland'; 'Enziandom'; 'Europa'; 'Générale Vicomtesse de Vibraye'; 'Geoffrey Chadbund'; 'Hamburg'; 'Kasteln'; 'King George'; 'Kluis Superba'; 'Le Cygne'; 'Madame Faustin Travouillon'; 'Maréchal Foch'; 'Merritt's Supreme'; 'Miss Hepburn'; 'Pink Lace'; Pink Shira™; 'Princess Beatrix'; 'Princess Juliana'; and 'Tovelit'.

HOW TO PRESERVE HYDRANGEAS

16

Drying Hydrangeas Successfully

When To Harvest

As with cut flowers, timing is everything. The height of summer is too soon because hydrangeas need to start the process of drying out themselves before they are ready for a successful harvest. During the summer they are still full of moisture. How can you tell when the time is right? You can literally feel when the flower heads are ready. Rest your hand lightly on the top of the flower and, if ready for harvest, it will feel papery, not soft and pliant as it feels in mid-summer. Another clue that the flower is ready for drying is that the "eye" in the center of the flower has exploded into a kind of starburst shape. To learn to recognize this, look at hydrangea flowers in the middle of the summer. All of the

In early October on Cape Cod the burgundy mopheads in the foreground are ready to be harvested for drying.

Notice the exploding "eye" in the center of the flower in the lower left area of this photo. The more starbursts you see on the flower, the more confident you should be that the flower is ready to be harvested.

eyes will be tight and rounded at that time of year. Sometimes new fresh flowers appear on a shrub late in the season. When you rest your hand on these you can feel how much softer they are than the mature blooms. Hold off on harvesting these late bloomers; they need time to mature on the shrub before being suitable candidates for drying. It is usually safe to begin harvesting in September, but let your sense of touch be your guide. If a flower feels very soft, it is probably not ready. You want the flowers to be dry when you harvest them so wait a few days after heavy rain. A day following a dry windy day would produce good results.

How to Harvest

Long stem method. Put two inches of water in the bottom of a bucket, have handy another container for the leaves you will be stripping off, and set both containers next to the first shrub to be harvested. The reason for the two inches of water in the bucket is to help the flower retain its shape as it dries. There is no need to replace the water when it eventually evaporates.

Begin removing flowers, cutting the stems as long as needed for the intended use. You will notice some stems on the shrub have no flowers at all; just foliage. Don't cut these; they are the stems that will bear flowers the following year.

Make the cut just above a node at an angle. A node is the place where new growth forms. It will look like small tight green growth. The reason for cutting just above a node is mainly aesthetic. Cutting too far above a node doesn't affect the flower's ability to dry or the health of the plant. It does, however, leave a bare stick which is unsightly.

Completely process each stem before cutting the next. This involves stripping off all the leaves, including the tiny ones right under the flower head. (You can snap them off with your hand; they come off quite easily.) Study the flower for any signs of damage, like sections that have been scorched by the sun. Pinch out these damaged sections. It is good to remove damaged sections at this time when the flower still retains some flexibility. If you wait until after it has dried it will be more brittle and you can accidentally pull off more than you intended to. Finally, run your hand gently over the flower to fluff it so that parts of it that may have been beaten down by the weather reclaim their rightful place. Place the stem in the bucket of water and move on to the next stem.

When placing the stems in the bucket, try to make sure the flowerheads are not pressing against each other. Staggering the height of the stems in the bucket helps to keep them separate. If too many flowerheads are crammed too tightly together, the resulting dried flowers will be misshapen. Aim for good air circulation around each flowerhead. This will assist in faster drying.

Once you have harvested all the stems you want, clean up the area, put the leaves on your compost pile, and bring the bucket of blooms inside to dry. Note: there is no rule that all your flowers to be dried have to be harvested on the same day. Staggering the harvest over several days, or even weeks, can yield a wider variation in color.

Short stem method. If you are drying flowers to be used in fashioning wreaths or other projects for which longer stems are not necessary, you can simply cut off the flower, just above a node, remove any leaves attached to this short stem, and place it in a tray. The author uses the kind of plastic

Short stems are separated by color for use in making wreaths.

mesh trays available at some garden centers for carrying home purchased plants. This kind of tray provides good air circulation and the trays can be easily stacked, once the flowers have dried. An advantage to this system is that you can place the flowers in trays according to color, making it easier to find the color(s) you need when making your wreath.

Where to Dry Hydrangeas

Place the bucket of harvested stems (or trays of flowers with short stems) in a warm, dark, and dry location. Of the three conditions, it is more important that the location be dark and dry.

- **Warm.** Hydrangeas placed in a warm location will dry faster than those placed in a cooler location. Faster drying is preferable for preserving colors. Since heat rises, attics are often good places for drying flowers as are the rafters of barns.

- **Dark.** The goal is to keep the flowers away from sunlight which makes the colors fade. You don't have to have a photo lab quality darkroom for drying your flowers; a dark corner of a room is fine.

- **Dry.** This is the most important condition. Avoid any place with high humidity like a laundry room where the humidity is periodically high. Too much dampness will disrupt successful drying.

Air Drying Method

Hydrangeas can also be air dried either by hanging them upside down (usually in small bunches), or right side up, provided the flowerheads are supported. If hanging upside down, bundle them together with a strong rubber band, making sure the heads of the flowers are spaced apart so they won't press against each other while drying.

Other Drying Methods

Silica gel absorbs moisture. Hydrangeas placed on top of a layer of silica gel and then covered completely with the same material will dry in a sealed container (such as a deep cookie tin) in about four days. This is the best method for color retention but impractical for drying many hydrangeas at one time. The use of microwave ovens for drying is not recommended because of the danger of fires.

The author needed to find a large container in which to dry this exceptionally large blue mophead. A large Christmas tin that once held popcorn was wide enough for the job.

The flower was set in place on top of a layer of silica gel crystals, then more of the silica gel crystals were gently poured around and over the flower. The tin was periodically tapped lightly on the table to encourage settling of the crystals.

Small plastic food storage containers can also be used for drying with silica gel crystals. If the flowerhead is too large it can be divided into smaller florets.

There was enough room around the hydrangea in the tin to surround it with silica gel crystals.

Blue mopheads divided into smaller florets.

An inch or two of silica gel crystals should be poured into the bottom of the container before flowers are added.

Instant Dried Arrangements

If you have the time and the inclination on a day when you are harvesting hydrangeas you can create an arrangement that will dry on its own. It may take a little longer because you will need to think about flower placement, but once you have made the arrangement it can be instantly displayed while the flowers dry in place.

For an instant arrangement put two inches of water in the base of the selected container and proceed to add flowers with all leaves removed. The primary difference between saving blooms in a bucket of water for later use and placing them directly in the display container has to do with spacing: in the former you aim for good air circulation to help speed the drying process; in the latter you can place them together tightly because you don't have to worry about their final dried shape. So what if a bloom gets crushed between two neighboring blooms? As long as it fills that space attractively, it is not a problem. With less air circulation the arrangement will take longer to dry completely, but it can be displayed where you want it shortly after it is completed. Instant gratification!

The author uses this metal ladle to pour in the crystals but such a utensil isn't necessary; a paper cup slightly pinched in the center to form a pouring spout works just as well.

Hydrangea Varieties That Dry Well

Most hydrangea varieties will give you good dried results, but it is important to note that some dry better than others especially with respect to depth of color and color retention. Hydrangeas particularly known to dry well are: 'Alpenglühen'; 'Altona'; 'Ayesha'; 'Blaumeise'; 'Bouquet Rose'; 'Deutschland'; 'Enziandom'; 'Europa'; 'Gartenbaudirektor Kühnert'; 'Générale Vicomtesse de Vibraye'; 'Gertrude Glahn'; 'Goliath'; 'Hamburg'; 'Kasteln'; 'King George'; 'Kluis Superba'; 'Lilacina'; 'Madame Faustin Travouillon'; 'Maréchal Foch'; 'Merritt's Supreme'; 'Otaksa'; 'Paris'; 'Princess Beatrix'; 'Princess Juliana', 'Veitchii'; and 'Zaunkönig'.

To dry oakleaf hydrangeas pick them when they are just turning pink and dry them upright in two inches of water.

Climbing hydrangea flowers dry well as do the flowers of many paniculata varieties.

Some late August hydrangea flowers are in agreement with the sentiment on the sundial beneath them: "Grow old along with me, the best is yet to be".

HOW TO CREATE ATTRACTIVE DRIED HYDRANGEA DISPLAYS

17

Crafting with Dried Blossoms

Dried hydrangeas are used to decorate homes in many forms and through many seasons. Projects vary from simple wreaths to elaborate topiaries, with many variations in between.

How long the color lasts depends on where you display your project (a wreath hanging where the sun hits it will fade faster than one protected from the sun) and the hydrangea variety you selected to dry. Some dry better than others and some retain their color better than others. The more you experiment with the hydrangeas in your own garden, the better you will be able to predict longevity.

A straw wreath base surrounded by dried hydrangeas in many colors.

If you have the opportunity to do so, study dried hydrangea wreaths and floral arrangements for sale in gift shops to see what effects you particularly like. If you have ever had the experience of looking at something in a store and saying to yourself *I could do that!* you should absolutely try creating a project using dried hydrangeas. It is easy to do and very satisfying when you see the end result which can be amazingly beautiful.

You may be surprised at how many hydrangea blossoms are needed to complete one small project like a simple wreath. Be prepared to have on hand many more dried flowers than you think you will need.

Dried hydrangea wreaths can be expensive. It is not unusual to see them for sale in gift shops priced anywhere from forty to eighty dollars and most of that cost reflects labor and design skills. The cost of the materials (wreath base, wire, greening pins, and ribbon if desired) usually comes to less than ten dollars. The hydrangeas are free if you have plenty of them planted in your garden. The design skills can easily be acquired with practice. The time needed to complete a dried hydrangea wreath ranges from one to two hours, depending on the size of the wreath and how much time is spent selecting the blossoms to put in place. The satisfaction of producing your own beautiful creation is priceless.

Creating just one project with dried hydrangeas invariably leads to others. It also prompts the designer to plant more hydrangeas to increase available materials.

Wreath Making Decisions

The basics of wreath making are fairly straightforward, but many choices can be made by the wreath designer, including color scheme, size, shape, whether the project will include other materials besides hydrangeas, and whether the hydrangeas should be dried before or after the wreath is made. Possible additional materials

A wreath in soft shades of blue and green.

include a variety of dried flowers other than hydrangeas, ribbons, and natural materials like seashells.

Color scheme. Usually the color scheme is determined by the hydrangeas in the wreath designer's garden. The more varieties you have planted in your garden, the more choice you will have in color selection. If you have a variety of colors available you can

decide if you want the wreath to be uniform in color or if you prefer a tapestry effect with many colors mixed together.

Size. Wreath bases come in many sizes from tiny to very large. It is helpful to know where you want to hang your wreath before you buy the base. **Note:** the finished wreath will be bigger than the base because of the bulky dimensions of most hydrangea blossoms. Add at least an extra two inches all the way around when planning a good fit on a wall.

Wreath shape. Most wreath bases are circular, but specialty shapes are available as well. You might decide to make a square wreath or a heart-shaped wreath, if such bases are available to you.

Hydrangeas alone. Beautiful wreaths can be created with hydrangeas all by themselves. Whether you choose flowers that are all the same color or mix the colors, the end result can be both simple and stunning.

Hydrangeas with ornaments. Wired ribbon is probably the most common ornament. Other ornaments often have something to do with geography (seashells frequently accent Cape Cod hydrangea wreaths) or season (for example, white hydrangeas combined with red ornaments for a Christmas wreath). Many plant materials can be used to great effect. The author once saw a beautiful wreath combining blue hydrangeas with deep purple statice. Another effective combination involved hydrangeas that had dried to a deep burgundy accented with sprays of crape myrtle fruits that had been spray painted metallic gold. Walk around your garden to see what possibilities suggest themselves to you.

When to dry the hydrangeas. You can harvest the hydrangeas on one day and make the wreath a few days later after they have dried, or make the wreath with fresh flowers, letting them dry in place. If you choose the latter make sure you wait until the flowers have already started the drying process on the shrub. Late August and early September are usually good times to do this. Choosing the right time for you to make the wreath is a matter of available time and personal preference. If you plan to harvest a lot of hydrangeas on the same day you probably won't have the time to create a wreath on the spot. But if you want only one wreath and you have a couple of hours, you can assemble it outside from flowers you pick from the shrub(s). One advantage of this choice is that it is easier to fasten the hydrangeas to the wreath frame tightly, creating a dense effect, since the stems are still somewhat flexible. Hydrangeas that have dried completely are more brittle and can snap apart while you are attaching them to the wreath.

Materials Needed

- Wreath base made of straw
- Greening pins
- Craft wire
- Hydrangeas

Wreath base. A wreath made of straw is recommended and the directions in this chapter for assembling the wreath are based on using this material, but it is important to note that other type wreaths may also be used, such as grapevine wreaths and rigid metal wreaths. The type of base will determine how the flowers should be attached. Depending on the wreath frame, the flowers may need to be attached with a glue gun or with wire rather than with greening pins.

Straw wreaths can be found in craft stores and some garden centers. They are often covered in plastic. There is no need to remove the plastic from the straw before attaching the flowers if you plan to cover the base completely. These wreaths are available in many sizes from eight to twenty-four inches. A

Few materials are needed to make beautiful wreaths.

Greening pins can be reused from one season to another. When the first wreath fades, remove the flowers and the greening pins and start again with a new batch of flowers.

twelve inch straw wreath is a good size to start with because it is easy to work with and the end result can be achieved in about an hour.

Greening pins. The u-shaped pins used for attaching the flowers to the straw base are usually called greening pins but they may also be called floral pins. They are sold in craft stores and florist supply outlets, often in packages of fifty or one hundred. You will need about 80 greening pins for a twelve inch wreath.

Craft wire. Craft wire is sold in many weights. Find one that is 26-gauge (or close to that). The wire is used to fashion the hook from which the wreath will hang. You want a wire that is strong enough to support the finished wreath and light enough to work with easily. Some craft stores offer ready-made hooks that are simply inserted into the back of the wreath, but these are sometimes hard to find.

Hydrangea flowers. You may be surprised to discover how many hydrangea flowers are required to complete a wreath. Be sure to have on hand more flowers than you think you will need. This is not a concern when fashioning a wreath directly from your garden shrubs to the wreath, as long as your shrubs are filled with flowers.

How to Craft a Hydrangea Wreath

Step 1. Gather all materials at your work station. A waist-high work station is recommended, like a kitchen counter. If working in the garden, consider using an old ironing board which can be adjusted to a comfortable height.

Step 2. Fashion the hook from which the finished wreath will hang, using the craft wire. It is important to do this before adding flowers as you would crush some flowers if you tried to do it later. Wrap the craft wire around the straw base anywhere, create the hook by twisting it into an oval shape, then secure the shape

Test the hook you make by hanging it on your finger.

with additional twisting. Once you have a good size hook, anchor it in place with a greening pin. Test the security of the hook by hanging it on your finger. Aim for a hook that is on the back of the wreath near the top of the base. If not secured properly it will slide above the wreath. If you plan to cover the wreath completely with flowers, this isn't a problem because the attached flowers will conceal the hook. Some designers allow some of the straw base to show through and if this is the case for you the hook should not be visible above the wreath.

Step 3. Begin to attach the flowers. If the flowers are very large you may want to separate them into manageable size florets. Each flower or floret should have a short stem which is what will be anchored with the greening pin.

A member of the Cape Cod Hydrangea Society has begun making her wreath, covering the top of the wreath base first.

The completed wreath is lovely.

Place the flower on the top of the wreath. Secure it by pushing a greening pin into the base as far as it will go, over the stem and as close to the flower as you can. Place the next flower over the stem of the first flower and anchor it in place. The flowers will all be going in the same direction with the flower to the left and the stem to the right (or vice versa if you are left-handed). Repeat this process until you have circled the wreath. An easy progression is to go all around the top, then all around the inside, then all around the outside of the wreath base.

Step 4. Attach ornaments if you so desire. Some ornaments, like ribbon, can be attached with wire or floral picks. Others, like seashells, can be hot-glued to the wreath.

Step 5. Hang the wreath where it will not be exposed to direct sunlight. Sunlight will fade the colors. The colors will eventually fade no matter where you place it and at that point you can either remove all the flowers and greening pins and start again with the current season's flowers, or you can lightly touch up the colors using a floral spray.

Floral Sprays

Faded dried hydrangeas can be touched up with floral sprays, available at craft stores. It will note on the spray can that the contents are suitable for flowers. Make sure you work in a well ventilated area

Flowers that have faded to a parchment shade can be saved with the use of a floral spray.

The spray used on these flowers was Design Master Cranberry #713.

and protect surrounding surfaces. A light touch is recommended. Natural effects can be achieved by using two colors to provide depth of color by spraying lightly with one color, waiting until it dries, then spraying lightly with the second color. For blue flowers, use a light blue and a darker blue. For pinks, use light pink and a darker pink. For purples, use pale lavender and

This topiary was constructed in very little time and has been on display in the author's home for years.

medium purple. Heavy saturation is not recommended as it leads to an unnatural effect. A wide variety of colors is available to suit any preference including colors called Larkspur Blue, Wedgwood Blue, French Blue, Blue Sky, Baby Blue, Hydrangea Blue, Delphinium Blue, Lilac, Hydrangea Green, Basil, Fresh Green, Wild Rose, and Cranberry. (Cranberry is a wonderful color to use for flowers used as Christmas accents.)

How to

Craft a Topiary

Dried hydrangeas with their long sturdy stems make ideal materials for topiaries. For this project you will need a heavy container as the base, floral foam, twist ties, wired ribbon, two long and straight hydrangea stems with flowers, and several short stems with smaller flowers.

Step 1. Fill the base with floral foam so that it fits inside the base snugly.

Step 2. Cut one long hydrangea stem to the desired height of the completed topiary. This is Stem A. Cut the second long stem to be slightly more than half the height of the first. This second one is Stem B.

Step 3. Insert Stem B, the shorter of the two long hydrangea stems, into the floral foam, centering it in the container.

Step 4. Ease the longer stem (Stem A) into the flower of the shorter stem to center it as best you can, then slide the stem down and into the floral foam as close as possible to the first stem. Use twist ties to secure the stems together under each of the two flowers. Cover the twist ties with wired ribbon cut to the desired length.

Step 5. Insert short stems to cover the floral foam at the base of the container, creating the third level of the topiary.

Dried Hydrangeas

in Containers

Dried hydrangeas make wonderful arrangements in vases and other containers, either alone or with other dried flowers. Selecting containers for dried flower arrangements is an enjoyable part of the creative process. Because hydrangea stems are not too attractive, opaque containers work well, emphasizing the flowers while hiding the stems. Solid color containers, especially blue, white, and pewter, seem to bring out the best in both fresh cut hydrangeas and dried hydrangeas. Baskets of all shapes and sizes make natural containers for dried arrangements.

Arrangements can be made while the hydrangeas are still fresh, provided you harvest them late in the season when they have begun the process of drying on the shrub(s). Put two inches of water in the base of your container before starting. This will help the flowers keep their shape while they finish drying. There is no need to replace the water as it evaporates.

Holiday Uses
of Dried Hydrangeas

Holidays, especially Christmas, bring out creative urges. Dried hydrangea blossoms can be used to create swags for stairways and mantelpieces. They can be used in their natural colors or enhanced with floral sprays. Cranberry and gold are popular choices if floral sprays are desired.

Years ago the author hung a decoration in the shape of a Christmas tree on a wall and decorated it with Christmas ornaments. The tree shape looked good there, inspiring a year round use for it. When the Christmas ornaments were removed, short stems of dried hydrangeas in their natural colors were inserted. Other dried flowers were added as filler. The end result was lovely – a kind of floral tree – and suited all seasons. The flowers faded by Christmas at which point it was appropriate to remove the dried flowers and decorate for Christmas again, continuing the cycle.

Once you start working with the materials, more ideas will probably pop into your head, especially if you have a lot of blooms to work with. It is hard to go wrong when working with such beautiful natural materials.

HOW TO FIND HYDRANGEA DISPLAYS

Enjoying Beautiful Hydrangeas in Garden Settings

18

Hydrangea display gardens around the world offer the enthusiast wonderful learning opportunities. A well organized display garden includes a substantial number of varieties all carefully chosen, organized, and labeled. Visitors are encouraged to wander around the flower beds taking notes of the varieties they love.

Plant collections are valuable both for reference and for plant preservation. Gardeners are familiar with the way certain plants wax and wane in popularity. Countless varieties have been lost over time when their popularity faded. Collections assure that different varieties will survive no matter what is happening in the commercial plant world.

The value of hydrangea collections for those who love this genus cannot be overestimated. It is immeasurably more instructive to see a plant yourself, than to see a picture of the plant. Often in a natural setting like this a certain plant will make you stop in your tracks. You will check the label to find out what this wonderful specimen is called. You wonder if it might be available at a garden center near where you live and, if not, how you can acquire it. You want to know if its blooms last for a long time and if it makes a good cut flower and whether it dries well. Because you want to know everything about it, your research becomes focused, the way people learn best.

The Shamrock Collection

With more than 1200 varieties the Shamrock Collection is the largest collection of hydrangeas in the world. It is located in the Normandy region of France in Varengeville-sur-Mer, where research is conducted involving identification of plants, comparisons of the various cultivars' growing behaviors, and the introduction of new varieties.

The information obtained is then disseminated internationally. The collection, founded by Robert and Corinne Mallet in 1984, has been designated the French National Collection and was named "The Shamrock Collection" in homage to Ireland where hydrangeas look so much at home.

The hydrangea varieties are arranged by country and region with each plant bed dedicated to one plant breeder. The Shamrock Collection has been described as a

A restful spot from which to view a portion of the Shamrock Collection.

Hydrangeas in a wide variety of colors are displayed in the Shamrock Collection.

Attention-getting blue mopheads, part of the Shamrock Collection.

living museum of the genus. Some of the specimens are the only ones known in the West; most of these were collected by Corinne Mallet in Japan.

The location of the Shamrock Collection, on the upper coast of Normandy, has the perfect temperate climate for hydrangeas. (Its climate is roughly like that found in the coastal regions of the state of Washington in the United States.) The long flowering season lasts from June to November with the collection open to the public from mid-June to mid-September.

With varieties carefully labeled and Corinne and Robert frequently on the scene to answer questions, it is the ideal place to learn about hydrangeas.

Holehird Gardens

Holehird is the home of the Lakeland Horticultural Society and is the site of the United Kingdom's largest national collection of hydrangeas with 14 species and over 200 cultivars. Most of the cultivars are located in the area called "Hydrangea Walk", with about 150 cultivars on display. The plants are arranged in such a way that visitors can see them from many angles. The overall impression is of plants flowing together, but labels are placed where the connection between plant and label is obvious. Proper

A tapestry of color in the hydrangea collection at Holehird Gardens located in the Lake District of England.

The plants are healthy and lush in Holehird's hydrangea collection.

Hydrangeas thrive in the climate of the Lake District in Windermere.

Blue lacecaps at Holehird Gardens resemble a mountain stream cascading downhill.

labeling is vital; if you see a plant you love you want to make sure you know its name so you can track it down elsewhere. Great care has been taken at Holehird, and other well maintained display gardens, to label plants accurately.

The ideal time to visit Holehird Gardens is mid-summer, to see the mopheads and lacecaps at their best. If you are there in June make sure you see the magnificent climbing hydrangea clinging to the stone above the archway just outside the walled garden.

Collection of the Cape Cod Hydrangea Society

With its mild coastal climate, Cape Cod is known for its lush and healthy hydrangeas. Recognizing its ideal situation, the Cape Cod Hydrangea Society began a collection of hydrangeas both as an educational resource and as a beautiful tourist destination at Heritage Museums and Gardens in Sandwich, Massachusetts. This display garden was planted with fifty varieties in its first year (2008) and had doubled its collection by 2011, with plans to add to the collection annually. The early collection concentrated on the macrophyllas (mopheads and lacecaps), but many other species are well represented including paniculatas, serratas, quercifolias, and arborescens. For a beautiful and ever-expanding display in a lovely garden setting, this collection should not be missed.

The white flowers of *Hydrangea arborescens* 'Annabelle' surround the sign pointing toward the hydrangea collection of the Cape Cod Hydrangea Society.

Hydrangea macrophylla 'Decatur Blue' catches the eye at the collection of the Cape Cod Hydrangea Society at Heritage Museums and Gardens in Sandwich, Massachusetts.

Hydrangea Farm Nursery

The island of Nantucket is also known for beautiful hydrangeas, not surprisingly since hydrangeas love to be near the water. Owners Mal and Mary Kay Condon have created a fabulous destination garden surrounding their farmhouse not far from Nantucket's town center. Their hydrangea farm is both a display garden, with lush plantings in curved flower beds throughout the grounds, and a retail operation where healthy plants can be purchased on the spot. With hundreds of varieties to admire and inspire, this is a popular area attraction.

The author fell in love with 'Brestenberg' while touring the hydrangea farm and subsequently planted this variety in honor of the birth of her granddaughter, Charlotte Maisie.

Pine trees frame the beautiful garden beds at Mal and Mary Kay Condon's Hydrangea Farm Nursery on the island of Nantucket.

H.m. 'Brestenberg' is only one of many beautiful hydrangeas to see at the Condons' Hydrangea Farm.

Maritime Regions

Many of the world's most beautiful hydrangea collections are located near water: the Shamrock Collection in the Normandy region of France, Holehird Gardens in the Lake District of England, and Cape Cod and the islands of Nantucket and Martha's Vineyard in Massachusetts among others. Hydrangeas thrive in these locations because they have a similar climate to Japan where most hydrangeas originated.

Japan

Japan is a wonderful travel destination for hydrangea lovers. Most hydrangeas originated in Japan's maritime climate and they are a very popular plant in that region. During the months of June and July hydrangea festivals throughout Japan celebrate the hydrangea (locally called "ajisai") in its many forms and colors. Parks, shrines, and temples are some of the locations for festivals, but they are not confined to contained areas like these. The Hakone Tozan Railway, for example, with trains running from Odawara Station to Gora Station offers views of over ten thousand hydrangeas. In Japan, hydrangeas are second only to their cherished cherry blossoms in popularity.

H.m. 'Nikko Blue' is a popular blue mophead on Cape Cod. This scene is in the garden of Joan Brazeau, the president of the Cape Cod Hydrangea Society.

Notable Hydrangea Collections
Throughout the World

AUSTRALIA

George Tindale Memorial Gardens,
    Sherbrooke, Victoria
Royal Botanic Gardens, South Yarra, Victoria

BELGIUM

Arboretum Kalmthout
Hydrangeum, The Collection of the
    Belgian Hydrangea Society, Destelbergen

CANADA

The University of British Columbia Botanical Garden,
    Vancouver, British Columbia
VanDusen Botanical Garden, Vancouver, British
    Columbia

ENGLAND

Darley Abbey Park, Derby
Dunham Massey, Cheshire
Hidcote Manor Garden,
    Chipping Camden, Gloucestershire
Holehird Gardens, Lake District, Windermere
Royal Botanic Gardens, Kew
Royal Horticultural Society's Garden, Wisley
Sir Harold Hillier Gardens, Romsey, Hampshire
Trebah Garden, Cornwall
Trelissick, Cornwall

FRANCE

Parc du Bois des Moutiers, Varengeville-sur-Mer
Shamrock Collection, Varengeville-sur-Mer

GERMANY

Mainau Island, Bodensee

IRELAND

John F. Kennedy Arboretum, New Ross,
    County Wexford, Ireland

JAPAN

Ajisai-en, Hydrangea garden in
    Motobu area of northern Okinawa.
Amabiki Kannon, Near Makabe.
Hakone Tozan Railway, trains between Odawara
    Station and Gora Station in Hakone with over
    10,000 hydrangea blooms along the railroad.
    Kanagawa.
Hakusan Jinja Shrine and Hakusan Koen Park,
    Bunkyo Hydrangea Festival, Bunkyo-ku, Tokyo.
Hasedera Temple, Hydrangea Pathways, Kamakura.
Hondoji Temple, 63 Hiraga Matsudo-city, Chiba.
Kaisei Town, Kanagawa Prefecture.
Kobe Forest Botanical Garden, Yamada-cho
    Kamidanigani Kita-ku Kobe-city, Hyogo.
Kyodo-no-Mori Museum, Fuchu-city, Tokyo.
Meigetsuin, Kanagawa.
Mimurotoji Temple Ajisai Garden,
    21 Todo-shigatani Uji-city, Kyoto.
Ohirasan Jinja Shrine, Hirai-cho Tochigi-city, Tochigi.
Osaka Fumin-no-mori (Osaka Prefectural Nature
    Parks), 2030-6 Yamatecho
    Higashi-Osaka-city, Osaka.
Rikugien Garden, Komagome Bunkyo-ku, Tokyo.
Sanzen-in Temple, famous for its garden.
    Located in Ohara, a village north of Kyoto.
Shimoda Ajisai Matsuri, Shimoda Koen Park,
    3-1174 Shimoda-city, Shizuoka.
Taiho Hachiman Shrine, Shimotsuma.
Takahata Fudoson, Takahata Hino-city, Tokyo.
    Toshima-en, Kouyama Nerima-ku, Tokyo.

NEW ZEALAND

Auckland Regional Botanic Gardens,
    Manurewa, Auckland.
Christchurch Botanic Gardens, Christchurch.
Woodleigh Gardens, New Plymouth.

SCOTLAND

Royal Botanic Gardens, Edinburgh.

SWITZERLAND

Basel Botanical Garden, Basel.

UNITED STATES OF AMERICA

Aldridge Gardens, Hoover, Alabama.
Atlanta Botanical Garden, Atlanta, Georgia.
Arnold Arboretum, Jamaica Plain, Massachusetts.
Brooklyn Botanical Garden, Brooklyn, New York.
Chicago Botanic Garden, Glencoe, Illinois.
Heritage Museums and Gardens,
    Sandwich, Massachusetts.
Hydrangea Farm Nursery, Nantucket, Massachusetts.
JC Raulston Arboretum, Raleigh, North Carolina.
Memphis Botanical Garden, Memphis, Tennessee.
The Morton Arboretum, Lisle, Illinois.
Norfolk Botanical Garden,
    Kaufman Hydrangea Collection, Norfolk, Virginia.
The Scott Arboretum of Swarthmore College,
    Swarthmore, Pennsylvania.
United States National Arboretum, Washington, D.C.
The University of Georgia Botanical Garden,
    Athens, Georgia.
Washington Park Arboretum,
    University of Washington, Seattle, Washington.
Winterthur Museum and Gardens,
    Winterthur, Delaware.

WALES

Bodnant Garden, Colwyn Bay, Clywd.

The view from this house is of Wychmere Harbor in Harwich, Massachusetts.

The author would love to hear from hydrangea enthusiasts who have discovered lovely displays of hydrangeas not mentioned above. She will be happy to include them in the appropriate page on her website, www.hydrangeamania.com.

Heavenly blue hydrangeas can be spotted all around Cape Cod and the islands.

Hydrangeas line this Orleans, Massachusetts, driveway near Arey's Pond.

Hydrangeas add the blue accent at an Independence Day celebration at this home in Harwich, Massachusetts.

Allen Harbor Yacht Club, Harwich Port, Massachusetts.

A waterfront home in Harwich, Massachusetts.

Go confidently in the direction of your dreams.

Live the life you have imagined.

~ Henry David Thoreau

A sign near a display of hydrangeas at the Wychmere Harbor Club in Harwich, Massachusetts.

The most common questions about hydrangeas have to do with lack of flowers, flower color, when and how to prune them, where to plant them, how to take care of them once planted, cutting flowers for fresh or dry uses, foliage problems, and requests for hydrangea recommendations. See below for answers to specific questions. Keep in mind these are the frequently asked questions. If you don't see your question addressed here, go to the chapter that deals specifically with that topic; your concern could very well be cleared up in the body of the text.

Why doesn't my hydrangea produce any flowers? (Usually when this question is asked, the person is referring to mophead or lacecap hydrangeas. This answer addresses the problem of lack of flowers on this species, *Hydrangea macrophylla.*)

An otherwise healthy looking hydrangea may not bloom for many reasons. The most common causes have to do with climate, improper pruning, too much shade, and overfertilization.

Hydrangeas flourish in U.S. Hardiness Zones 6-9. If you live in a colder climate your hydrangea might die back every winter meaning no flower buds survive the winter. Even in the recommended zones a late frost after a thaw can kill off the flower buds that have broken dormancy. Hydrangeas planted on the north or east side of the house fare better during late frosts because they break dormancy later than those planted in a southern exposure, keeping the flower buds protected longer.

Garden sites that are very windy can cause problems because the wind can dry out (and kill) the flower buds. A winter with a lot of snow is actually good for hydrangeas because the snow provides insulation from the drying effects of the wind.

On most mopheads and lacecaps the flower buds are set on old wood meaning stems that grew during the previous growing season. If you cut back your hydrangea in the fall you are removing flower buds at the same time. Waiting until spring to prune gives your flowers a better chance of survival.

Some sun is necessary for flowers to appear. Morning sun and afternoon shade is ideal. A hydrangea planted near a small tree may bloom for several years but when the tree grows larger casting more shade the hydrangea may not get the requisite hours of sunlight needed to produce flowers. High shade from deciduous trees or pines seems to allow enough sunlight through for good flowering; what you want to avoid is dense shade.

Excessive fertilizing can lead to lush foliage at the expense of flower production. It is a natural inclination to think adding plant food will help the plant bloom, but this is not the case. It is better to underfeed rather than overfeed hydrangeas.

If hydrangeas are planted adjacent to a lawn, and if that lawn is heavily fertilized with nitrogen, your hydrangeas might also be getting a burst of nitrogen which promotes green growth (foliage) but not flowers.

Some well established shrubs that consistently bloomed for years may suddenly stop producing flowers or the flowering will be sparse. Usually the reason can be traced back to the previous winter. Extremely cold winters with little snow to provide insulation might have killed back the old canes (those that would have produced flowers). The new canes, grown that year, can be filled with lush foliage giving the impression of a healthy plant, but these new canes haven't matured enough to produce flowers. Back-to-back cold winters with little snow can cut back flower production severely. You might want to provide winter protection for your hydrangeas, particularly if they are in a site where strong winds prevail.

Why doesn't my climbing hydrangea have any flowers?

Flowers on a climbing hydrangea appear with secondary growth. Secondary growth occurs after primary growth when the climbing hydrangea is busy scrambling up whatever is supporting it such as a garden shed, a trellis, or a tree. Most of the secondary growth appears *after* the climbing hydrangea has reached the top of a structure and can climb no further. Some secondary growth may appear at the lower levels before the climb is completed. This is why you might see some flowers at the base of a tree but not further up. You must be prepared for delayed gratification when planting a climbing hydrangea. The shorter the climb, the faster the gratification. You will see flowers earlier on a climbing hydrangea planted at the base of a six-foot trellis than on one planted at the base of a forty-foot tree.

How can I change the color of my hydrangea?

Hydrangeas are really remarkable in the plant world with their ability to change flower color. When the plant absorbs aluminum from the soil the flowers are blue. If aluminum is not present in the soil or if the plant cannot absorb it the flowers are pink. The plant is able to absorb aluminum in an acidic soil which usually prevails throughout an entire region which is why you will see mainly blue hydrangeas on Cape Cod. An alkaline soil, which is most prevalent in large parts of California and in England, blocks the absorption of aluminum and in these parts of the world most hydrangea flowers are pink. Acidic soils and alkaline soils are at opposing ends of the pH scale. If your garden soil falls in a neutral range – neither very acidic nor very alkaline – a wide range of hydrangea flower colors is possible.

If you want to change the color of your hydrangea flowers from blue to pink or from pink to blue you need to add products to the soil: aluminum sulfate (for blues) or lime (for pinks). Do not expect instant results. It is easier to control the pH of the soil in a container than in the garden.

It should be noted that you cannot change the color of white hydrangeas. Mother Nature may change them by way of the aging process, but you will not be able to make a white hydrangea flower turn blue or pink.

When using either aluminum sulfate or lime, make sure you follow the package directions. Too much can be toxic to the plant.

I saw a hydrangea for sale called 'Nikko Blue', but the flowers were pink. The people at the garden center assured me it was labeled correctly and that the flowers would be blue in my garden. It doesn't seem possible. Are they right?

Commercial potting soils are neutral on the pH scale and tend to produce pink hydrangea flowers. The growers usually add soil amendments to make sure the flowers of certain varieties are blue at point of sale, but it is not always done. This is why you may see a *pink* 'Nikko Blue' for sale at a garden center. Once 'Nikko Blue' is planted in acidic soil and aluminum from the soil is absorbed, the flowers will gradually turn blue. Assuming you have acidic soil in your area, the advice you got is correct; this hydrangea will eventually be a medium shade of blue.

I moved my blue hydrangea to another part of my garden and now the flowers are pink. Why? What can I do to make the flowers blue again?

It is really interesting to see this happen. A hydrangea shrub might produce blue flowers for many years but the first flowers following transplanting are very likely to be pink. Once the plant has settled into its new location and can tap into the aluminum in the soil, the flowers will turn blue again. Once reestablished, the blue flowers should appear reliably year after year. If blue flowers are really important to you, add aluminum sulfate to the soil in the spring.

My blue hydrangeas are turning to pink. I have had them for years and they have always been blue. What's going on? What should I do?

The usual reason for blue hydrangeas to turn pink is that lime has been added to the soil. Presuming you haven't transplanted them from one part of your garden to another (which can cause a temporary change from blue to pink), I suspect lime is affecting the soil near your hydrangeas. If your shrubs are planted right next to your lawn, and if you have added lime to your lawn, some of the lime may have leached over to your shrubs, affecting the flower color. If this is the case, you need do nothing. Just take more care when applying lime to your lawn in the future so it won't happen again. As a countermeasure you could also consider adding aluminum sulfate to the soil around your shrubs in the spring.

Everyone who lives near me grows blue hydrangeas so I thought mine would be blue too but they are not, they are pink. What should I do to make them blue? Did I just get the wrong kind?

For hydrangea flowers to turn blue they need to absorb aluminum from the soil. If you have an alkaline soil, the absorption of aluminum is blocked and your flowers remain pink. A logical starting point for you is to have your soil tested. Garden centers sell test kits. You can also consult your local master gardeners to find out how to get your soil tested. If you do this and learn your soil is not alkaline but acidic, the problem may be that there is insufficient aluminum in the soil around your plant. In the spring as the buds are forming apply aluminum sulfate to the soil according to package directions. It is important to note that some (but not many) hydrangea varieties resist color changes. One is 'Alpenglühen' that tends to stay pink regardless of the pH of the soil. This is not to say that it won't turn blue, but it resists the change. If you have this variety and you really want blue flowers you might want to add another hydrangea to your garden making a point of selecting one known to produce blue flowers in an acidic soil.

My neighbor gave me three baby plants she grew from cuttings she took from her beautiful blue hydrangea bush. She did this as a favor to me because she knows I love those flowers. My baby plants had a few flowers and they were all pink, not blue. What should I do?

Wait. Really. Baby plants from hydrangeas with blue flowers often show pink flowers the first year they are in the ground. The roots need to get established so they can absorb the aluminum needed to turn the flowers blue. If the flowers are still pink after a few seasons planted in your garden, you will need to add aluminum sulfate around the plants to help get the blue color you desire, until the plant produces the blue color naturally.

I specifically bought a hydrangea plant with deep pink flowers. Everyone in this area has blue flowers but I prefer the pink ones. The first year in the ground it looked wonderful, especially because that color was chosen to complement some other plants in the area. But now it seems to be changing color. Some of the flowers are still pink but others are lavender and others are blue. Why is it doing that and what should I do to make the flowers pink again?

You probably live in an area with acidic soil, given the fact that you see blue hydrangeas all around you. Hydrangea flowers will be blue in acidic soil and pink in alkaline soil. To return your hydrangea to the pink you prefer, you need to add dolomite lime to the soil, following package directions. You will need to do this every year to prevent the flowers from becoming blue.

What is the name of the hydrangea that has green flowers?

This is a tricky question to answer without knowing the species you have in mind and what time of year you are seeing these green flowers. Three different species can produce green flowers: macrophyllas (mopheads and lacecaps); arborescens; and paniculatas.

Some mopheads and lacecaps turn green as the flowers mature in the fall. A flower that was blue during the summer might be green in September and October.

Many arborescens varieties, with 'Annabelle' a good example, start off with green flowers in the spring. These flowers eventually turn pure white and remain white through most of the growing season, but then they revert to green in the fall.

Some paniculata varieties, notably 'Limelight' and Little Lime™, have distinctive green flowers before they turn white (then pink and burgundy in the fall).

There is a *Hydrangea serrata* which is said to produce green flowers, but not consistently. The variety is called 'Midori yama'. The word "midori" in Japanese means green and "yama" means mountain.

I bought a hydrangea that is supposed to have deep purple flowers which is exactly what I want. But the flowers aren't purple at all, they are pink. Can you recommend a variety that has deep purple flowers?

You probably already have the right plant in your garden. What you don't have is the right soil. Deep pink flowers turn deep purple or deep blue in an acidic soil. Since your flowers are pink, you must have an alkaline or neutral soil. You need to amend your soil with aluminum sulfate to give your flowers a chance to turn purple. This is not likely to happen quickly in garden soil. It is easier to control colors with plants in containers than those planted in the garden.

The label on the hydrangea I bought said it was one of the best purples. I really wanted a purple hydrangea but the flowers are deep pink. Was the plant mislabeled or did I do something wrong?

A plant label at a garden center can sometimes cause confusion, not because of what it says but because of what it doesn't say. The information it contains can be accurate but mislead because it leaves out a vital point. For instance, the author once found a label on a hydrangea that said to plant it in sun or shade. It did *not* warn that most hydrangeas planted in deep shade will have no flowers, nor did it say that the flowers of hydrangeas planted in full sun will fade faster than those planted in the ideal conditions: morning sun and afternoon shade.

As to the label on your plant about purple flowers, it may well be that your plant will give you purple flowers *if your soil is acidic*. This is a crucial omission. It would have been better if it had said: *purple in acidic soil; pink in alkaline soil.* Then you would have known to ask how you could tell which soil you have and what to do if it is not what you want. In your case you probably need to add aluminum sulfate to the soil.

I want hydrangea flowers in a rich purple color. Which one should I get?

I can tell you the name of some varieties that yield purple flowers *in an acidic soil*. The last few words of that sentence are very important. If you live in an area where pink hydrangeas predominate, you will have to add aluminum sulfate to the soil to achieve purple flowers. Some lovely purple mophead varieties include 'Merritt's Supreme'; 'Purple Majesty'; 'Europa'; 'Mathilda Gutges'; and 'Oregon Pride'. If you want purple lacecaps look for 'Geoffrey Chadbund'; 'Nightingale'; 'Kardinal'; and 'Mousmé'.

Can you recommend a good pink hydrangea?

One pink variety that resists color changes, even in an acidic soil where other pinks might turn blue, is 'Glowing Embers' (which is also called 'Alpenglühen'). It is a rich deep pink color. Over time in an acidic soil it may turn blue, in which case you would need to add lime to the soil to get pink blooms again. Other good pinks include 'Big Daddy','Haworth Booth', 'Kasteln', 'King George', and 'Masja'.

How can I make my pale blue hydrangea a deep blue?

Hydrangea varieties have a tendency toward color intensity; some tend to be pale, some a medium shade, and some a deep shade. Your pale blue hydrangea is not likely to change to deep blue no matter what you do. It is programmed to be a pale shade. The best you can do is to give it good growing conditions, as a healthy plant will yield the best possible color in its range. Over time in ideal conditions some medium blue hydrangeas turn a deeper blue. This tendency has been noted particularly in maritime climates. If you want deep blue hydrangea flowers the best thing to do is to acquire a variety known to produce this color.

Some of the best varieties for deep blue flowers are 'Altona', 'Blue Danube', 'Enziandom', and 'Hamburg'. Adding aluminum sulfate to the soil in the spring will encourage the flowers to be the best blue they can be.

I saw a hydrangea that had a lot of different color flowers on the plant at the same time. What kind of hydrangea is it?

At what time of year did you see this? It is common in the early hydrangea blooming season to see mopheads and lacecaps sporting many colors at the same time before they settle into the overall solid color they will show for most of the growing season. In this kind of situation you will see flower heads in many different colors and sometimes many colors on the same flower head. It is a beautiful and striking effect.

A few hydrangea varieties are known to produce many colors simultaneously, not just when the flowers first appear but well into the growing season. The best known examples are 'Mathilda Gutges' and 'Parzifal'.

It is also possible that unusual circumstances produced multicolored flowers on shrubs that previously produced a single color flower. Usually on Cape Cod hydrangea colors are blue. One summer, however, after a winter of record snowfall (over 100 inches), many shrubs that normally produced blue flowers were covered with multicolored blooms. One hypothesis for this phenomenon was that melting snow washed away a lot of aluminum in the sandy soil. The flowers need to absorb aluminum to turn blue.

Some people like to play with hydrangea colors in containers. Picture a single mophead hydrangea planted in the middle of a square container. If aluminum sulfate (mixed according to package directions) is applied to the soil in two opposite corners and lime is applied to the other two opposite corners, you may end up with a hydrangea sporting many colors at the same time.

This year for the first time I had one flower on my hydrangea bush that had a lot of different colors in it. Why did this happen? Will it happen from now on?

I suspect the rest of the flowers were blue. All but one of the flowers were able to absorb all the aluminum they needed from the soil to turn blue. One flower somehow got some aluminum (causing part of the flower to turn blue) but not enough (causing other parts to turn lavender or pink). It is a fluke and isn't likely to occur consistently year after year. It is interesting when it happens, though, like seeing a rainbow on some, but not all, rainy days.

When should I prune my hydrangeas?

Some hydrangeas bloom on old wood and some on new wood and this is a factor that must be taken into consideration. To be clear on pruning you need to understand the difference.

"Old wood" means wood (stems and branches) that grew during the previous growing season. All varieties in the macrophylla species (mopheads and lacecaps) bloom on old wood. (Some also bloom on new wood. Reblooming

mopheads and lacecaps will bloom on both old and new wood. If flower buds are inadvertently removed in the fall, or if a killing frost zaps the emerging buds in the spring, the shrub will still produce flowers on the new growth. To encourage a second flush of flowers on rebloomers, remove flowers from the shrub as they fade. See Chapter 7 for a list of rebloomers.) Oakleaf hydrangeas also bloom on old wood.

The flower buds for the next season are set after the current season's flowers put on their colorful display. If your hydrangeas are in full bloom in July, expect to see buds forming on newer stems from August on into the fall. You may cut back the stems bearing flowers, but not the stems bearing buds if you want flowers the following summer. The good news is that you don't have to prune at all in the summer or fall. Waiting to prune in the spring makes pruning decisions easy because you can see the fresh green growth from which stems and eventually flowers will appear and you merely need to cut out the dead sticks and old flowers appearing above the fresh growth. It is good to do this when the new growth is visible but still small because it makes it easier to see where cuts should be made.

Here is a general guideline for pruning hydrangeas: **when in doubt, don't prune at all**.

"New wood" refers to new growth that appeared in the current growing season. Both paniculatas and arborescens varieties produce flowers on new wood. The ideal time to prune these species is in the late winter or early spring when it is easy to see the structure of the plant. Each species can be cut back severely at this time, and

still grow back and flower beautifully later the same year. Prune arborescens varieties down to a foot to eighteen inches above the ground. Paniculatas should be pruned to just above a set of nodes. This could be as low as the lowest set of nodes on the plant but if frost damage is possible you could cut it above the second set of nodes from the ground. Please note, you don't have to prune either species at all, except to remove dead and otherwise unsightly branches. If you decide not to prune, the plant will eventually produce more flowers but the flowers will become progressively smaller. If you prune there will be fewer but larger flowers.

My hydrangea is becoming overgrown. How can I get it under control?

This is a common problem. When the plant is purchased at a garden center it is usually fairly small. When the gardener brings it home it seems logical to plant it next to a path or by the front door or under a window. But when the plant grows to the size it is programmed to be (most mopheads grow to five feet tall and just as wide) the plant might now be blocking the path or door or interfering with the view from the window. This is when relief is sought.

The best solution is to move the plant to a better location where its size is not a problem. It could then be replaced with a smaller hydrangea variety. (See Chapter 4 for recommendations.)

Otherwise the plant will have to be pruned regularly, possibly at the expense of flowers.

I'm assuming you have mophead hydrangeas. I would advise you not to prune at all until spring. Next spring, wait until fresh green growth appears then prune dead "sticks" at top of each shrub down to fresh green growth. If you prune in the fall you are removing potential flowers for next year. If you are more concerned about the size of the shrubs and are willing to sacrifice flowers, you can cut them down to a more manageable size, but I would still wait until the spring because pruning now would encourage new growth and that new growth is more tender and susceptible to winter damage. I need to point out that, even if you cut them back significantly, they will try to return, as quickly as possible, to the size they are programmed to be. In the case of the mopheads, most of them mature to about 5' tall by 5' wide. If that size is too big for the location, you might want to consider moving them.

If you prune at the wrong time of year you can be cutting off most of the flowers for the following year. You need to prune either right after flowering, before the plants set the buds for the following year, or wait until spring and just do a light pruning as outlined above.

How drastically should I cut my mopheads back?

Avoid cutting any hydrangea down to the ground. Young mopheads and lacecaps need no more than a light pruning to remove dead wood and flowers. Older mopheads and lacecaps can be rejuvenated by selecting a few old stems to remove completely. Do this every year until the plant is completely rejuvenated. Don't remove *all* the old stems at the same time as this can stress the plant. (You can easily identify the old stems; they are brown, not green, and usually thicker and more rigid than younger stems.)

When is the best time to plant a hydrangea?

Late spring and early fall are good times to plant hydrangeas. You can also plant in the summer but avoid very hot days or windy days when the plant can dry out easily. It is already stressed from the planting. If a series of cool rainy days are in the forecast during the summer, this is a good time to plant, provided you are prepared to keep a close eye on the plant's watering needs once warmer days return.

Should I plant my hydrangea in sun or shade?

Mopheads and lacecaps should ideally be planted in a situation with morning sun and afternoon shade.

Oakleaf hydrangeas can be planted in sun or shade but keep in mind that they bloom best with plenty of heat. Radiant heat from a foundation or driveway will encourage good blooming.

Paniculatas bloom best in sunny locations. You may need to provide some sun protection if you live in the south.

Climbing hydrangeas prefer the shade or partial shade but will bloom in the sun as well.

Arborescens varieties bloom in both sun and shade.

Are there some mopheads and lacecaps that tolerate shade better than others?

The following mopheads can tolerate shade but not dense shade; they need some dappled sun to flower well: 'Goliath'; 'Niedersachen'; 'Paris'; 'Frillibet'; 'Harlequin'; 'La France'; 'Nigra'; and 'Sister Theresa'.

Lacecaps that tolerate shade include 'Veitchii'; 'Beauté Vendômoise'; 'Lemon Wave'; and 'Mariesii Perfecta'.

Can I plant the hydrangea I got for Mother's Day?

Yes, by all means, but realize that hydrangeas that are forced for the potted trade are likely to be smaller and more tender (less cold hardy) than those grown for garden use. Winter protection for the first three years in the ground is recommended.

How much water does my hydrangea need?

Hydrangeas are happiest in an evenly moist, well-drained soil. It is better to water deeply once a week than just slightly on a daily basis. Weekly watering encourages deeper roots which will help sustain the hydrangea(s) during periods of drought. Mulch around the plant to help the area retain moisture.

What's the best fertilizer for hydrangeas?

An all-purpose balanced fertilizer is fine for hydrangeas. "Balanced" means all the numbers in the NPK ratio stated on the product label are the same, such as 10-10-10 or 14-14-14. If you are partial to either blue or pink flowers, other ratios are recommended. See Chapter 6 which addresses color issues.

Someone said I should protect my hydrangeas during the winter. How should I do this?

Winter protection is applied to hydrangeas that are more tender than others, in a colder climate than others, or in a garden site susceptible to cold winds. Plants may be tender if they are very young, if they were supplied by a florist for indoor use, or if the variety itself is known to be more tender than others. If, for any reason, you feel your plant may be vulnerable to harsh winter conditions, consider providing some protection.

Winter protection should be applied when the plant is dormant. Wait until all the leaves have dropped off the plant. In the northeast this often occurs by early December.

An easy way to insulate the plant is to surround it with chicken wire at a height that is taller than the plant. Secure the wire so that it won't tip over or come apart. Then fill the enclosure around the plant with pine needles or leaves. Pine needles are better because they don't compact as leaves tend to. Leave the protection in place until the spring when the first green growth appears.

How can I get my cut hydrangeas to look fresh for a long time when I make flower arrangements?

Make sure the flower is ready to be picked for indoor use. Early spring hydrangea flowers that have yet to fully develop their color, usually showing a mix of yellow in with their ultimate color, do not last very long as cut flowers. This is unfortunate as they can be quite lovely at that stage. If you want your flowers to last at least a week (and often longer) you need to wait until the color is fully developed.

If you can, water the plant well the night before you plan to cut some flowers. You want the flowers to be as full of water as possible and for that reason it is best to cut them early in the morning, even if you don't plan to arrange them until later in the day. Have a bucket of water to put them in immediately and strip off all the leaves. If you desire leaves in the arrangement, cut some stems with only leaves and not flowers.

Cut the stems at an angle and then make a vertical cut at the end of the stem with sharp scissors. This creates the right conditions for the flower stem to absorb the water needed to support the large flower head.

Condition the flowers as soon as you bring them indoors. You want to place them in water to which a floral preservative has been added and leave them in a cool location for a few hours. This gives the flowers time to recover from the stress of being cut. You can help them further by placing dampened white paper towels over the flowers.

Recut the stems when making your floral arrangement. The shorter the stem, the longer your flowers will look fresh.

If cutting hydrangeas for indoor use is important to you, consider planting one or more varieties known to be particularly good cut flowers. See Chapter 15 for a list of recommended plants.

When is the best time to harvest hydrangeas to dry?

You need to wait until the flowers have matured on the shrub and have started the process of drying already. The flowers will start to feel less soft and more papery. The time of year varies depending on geography. September is usually safe in the northeast and in the Pacific Northwest. It may be possible to dry them earlier in more southern areas.

What's the best way to dry hydrangeas?

Wait until the best time of year for harvesting (see preceding answer). Cut a stem to the length you want, pull off all the leaves, and place the stem in a bucket to which you have added two inches of water. Keep adding stems to the bucket and try to stagger the flower heads so that they are not resting against each other. Aim for good air circulation. You may need more containers if you want to dry a lot of hydrangeas. Next place the container(s) in a warm, dark, and dry location. The flowers dry faster in a warm environment than in a cold one. The area doesn't have to be completely dark; the point is to keep the flowers away from sunlight which can fade the colors. Avoid humid areas like a laundry room as this location is not conducive to good drying conditions. The flowers will dry fairly quickly, anywhere from just a few days to a week or so depending on when you picked them and what your drying conditions are.

Deep green veins in new leaves that are yellow are a sign of iron chlorosis.

Why are the leaves on my hydrangea turning yellow?

Four possible causes of yellow leaves are overwatering, powdery mildew, nitrogen deficiency, and iron chlorosis.

Overwatering your hydrangea may cause the leaves to turn yellow. Yellowing leaves signal that something is going wrong with the plant. A first step to diagnosis is to ease up on the watering to see if this helps the condition clear up.

Powdery mildew is a plant disease which first manifests itself as a white or light grey powdery-looking substance on the surface of the leaves. It is common on plants grown in the shade and in conditions of high humidity. It is an unattractive (but usually not lethal) condition that eventually causes leaves to turn yellow. The best treatment if the mildew becomes severe includes removing the infected leaves and spraying the shrub with a fungicide. A good preventative measure is to do whatever you can to increase air circulation around the plant.

When old leaves start turning yellow it may be a sign of **nitrogen deficiency**. If this is the cause you will likely see the condition showing up on the lower leaves first before it moves up to leaves located higher on the shrub. The yellow color will be uniform which distinguishes the cause from iron chlorosis. A plant suffering from a nitrogen deficiency can be treated with an application of a balanced fertilizer. Avoid applying a fertilizer in the fall, however, as this might promote new growth too tender to survive harsh winter conditions.

If you notice new leaves turning yellow *with green veins*, this is likely a sign of **iron chlorosis**. Treat with a chelated iron product obtained at a garden center. This condition is common in high pH soils. You can also try lowering the pH by applying aluminum sulfate and/or by mulching around the plant with pine bark or pine needles which eventually break down and lower the soil's pH.

There are holes on the leaves on my hydrangea. What's wrong?

The holes are probably caused by insects munching on the leaves. Sometimes you can catch them in the act. If you see the insects causing the damage, you can physically remove them from the plant. If you don't see them and if the damage is severe, treat the leaves with an insecticidal soap or spray with an insecticide. If the damage is mild (just one or two leaves affected), no treatment is necessary.

Occasionally holes are the result of branches dropping from trees located above the plants. Look to see if there are branches downed in the area. This may be the sole cause of leaf damage.

Why are my hydrangeas developing ugly spots on the leaves? What should I do?

Many leaf spots are fungal in nature. One called *cercospora hydrangeae* is most noticeable in the fall with symptomatic tan lesions with dark purple halos. Late summer rain can make the problem more severe. As with any fungal infection, it is important to keep the area clean. Pluck off diseased leaves and don't put them in the compost pile; get rid of them. When the plant loses all leaves in late fall, rake them up and dispose of them. When new leaves appear the following spring keep an eye on the plant for recurring symptoms and treat with a fungicide. If in doubt about whether what you are looking at is a fungus, bring the affected foliage to your university extension agent or to your local garden center for advice.

What are the best hydrangeas for a cold climate?

Hydrangeas that bloom on new wood are good choices for cold climates. These include Hydrangea arborescens varieties (like 'Annabelle') and varieties of Hydrangea paniculata. Because they bloom on stems grown during the current season, there are no concerns about winter die back or late frosts.

If you prefer a mophead or lacecap you are in luck. Recent breeding developments have led to the introduction of "remontant" hydrangeas, meaning hydrangeas that bloom on both old and new wood. They are also called "rebloomers". Some varieties of mopheads with this characteristic include the popular Endless Summer®, 'Penny Mac', 'David Ramsey', 'Decatur Blue', Endless Summer® 'Blushing Bride', and 'Oak Hill'. Twist-n-Shout® is a remontant (reblooming) lacecap.

I would like to plant a hydrangea in a corner where a screen porch meets the house. I love the big blue mophead type hydrangeas but want a variety which will be midsized, maybe 4' high. Can you recommend a variety that will have a long blooming season and meets my height requirement?

Most mophead varieties are about five feet tall at maturity and some are even taller. Some varieties tend to be around the four foot height you require, but please be aware that, if the hydrangea loves its conditions, it could grow taller than the norm. You didn't mention how much sunlight that particular location in your garden gets, and at what time of day. In general, morning sun and afternoon shade is best. The variety recommendations included here all *tend* to be on the short side, growing to about four feet tall and wide. **'All Summer Beauty'** has vivid blue flowers in an acidic soil and grows best in light shade. **'Amethyst'** has a frilly appearance to its flowers that are light blue (in acidic soil) when they first appear and darken as they age. **'Blauer Zwerg'** is known for months of bloom. Its name means "Blue Dwarf" and has a nice compact habit that works well in small gardens and in containers. **'Blue Danube'** is a dark blue in acidic soil with large flower heads. **'Böttstein'** is dark blue in an acidic soil with abundant flowers.

Can you tell me some good hydrangeas for a small garden?

Hydrangea breeders have been producing an increasing number of plants for small gardens in recent years. There are several new (and some old) varieties from which to choose.

The smallest **mopheads** include plants in the Cityline™ series including Berlin, Mars, Paris, Rio, Venice, and Vienna (the smallest of the series); the Halo Hydrangeas™ series (all bicolor) including Angel Eyes™ and Angel Smile™; 'Harlequin'; 'Hörnli'; 'Pia' (also known as Pink Elf®); Sabrina™; and Stella™.

Some mopheads that are generally in the 3'-4' range include 'All Summer Beauty'; 'Alpenglühen'; 'Amethyst'; 'Ami Pasquier'; 'Blauer Zwerg'; 'Blue Danube'; 'Böttstein'; 'Bouquet Rose'; 'Brunette'; 'Forever Pink'; 'Masja'; 'Merritt's Supreme'; Mini Penny™; 'Miss Belgium'; 'Purple Majesty'; 'Red Star'; 'Regula'; 'Tödi'; 'Tovelit'; and 'Trophée'.

Some smaller **lacecaps** include Angel Lace™; 'Izu-no-Hana'; 'Shamrock'; 'Sol'; and 'Zaunkönig'.

Petite **paniculatas** include 'Bombshell'; 'Dharuma'; 'Kyushu'; Little Lime™; 'Pee Wee'; and White Diamonds™.

If an **oakleaf** hydrangea is what you desire, look for 'Little Honey'; 'Pee Wee'; 'Ruby Slippers'; 'Munchkin'; and 'Sikes Dwarf'.

Hydrangea **arborescens** varieties generally range from three to six feet tall. 'Hayes Starburst' is at the smaller end of that scale.

Can I grow hydrangeas in pots on my deck? If so, which ones?

Hydrangeas make wonderful container plants. They provide big impact over a long period of time. All of the smaller varieties noted above would be perfectly suitable as container plants, but larger varieties can also work in containers, provided the containers are large enough. Certain hydrangea varieties are known to do very well in containers including 'Adria'; 'Altona'; 'Ami Pasquier'; 'Blauer Zwerg'; 'Blue Danube'; 'Compacta'; 'Forever Pink'; 'Harlequin'; 'Hörnli'; 'Masja'; 'Merritt's Supreme'; Mini Penny™; 'Miss Belgium'; 'Pia'; 'Pink Lace'; 'Tovelit'; and all varieties in the Cityline™ (Berlin, Paris, Rio, Venice, Vienna) series.

Deer are a problem in my garden. Are there any hydrangeas that are deer resistant?

Alas, no. While it is true that deer have observable food preferences and lists have been compiled with plants typically placed in categories (rarely damaged, seldom damaged, occasionally damaged, and frequently damaged), deer don't read these lists and browse plants based on need. Severe weather conditions such as deep snow and excessive cold encourage them to eat whatever they can find. They enjoy browsing on succulent growth in the spring. Deer population growth can lead to damage of plants not previously harmed. Regional differences seem to prevail as well. Garden forums on the Internet are full of contradictory advice. Someone in Ohio may have great luck with plant x ("Deer never bother it!"), while a gardener from Georgia might respond that plant x is the one plant the deer are most likely to eat. If deer are a problem for you, you will probably have to resort to one or more control measures.

What can I do to keep deer from eating my hydrangeas?

Several control measures are available. They include plant placement, repellents, frightening devices, and protective barriers.

Plant placement. Shrubs planted close to your house are less likely to get eaten than those on the perimeter of your property. If you have some hydrangeas under attack by deer, consider planting a protective ring around them of plants deer are known not to like, including buxus, berberis, daphne, potentilla, and buddleia.

Repellents. There are many commercially available repellents. They include contact repellents which are applied directly to plants causing them to taste bad and area repellents which are placed in the general area to repel with a foul odor. Think of these as taste deterrents and scent deterrents. Garden forums are full of advice about which are most effective, but there seems to be common agreement that alternating taste deterrents with scent deterrents works best.

Some home remedies include hot sauce, chicken eggs, and bars of soap hanging from trees.

Whatever repellents you decide to use, you must keep reapplying at regular intervals.

Frightening devices. These are used with the hope that if deer are startled sufficiently they will leave the garden promptly before snacking on plants. One of the most common is a motion detector that triggers a water spray. Others include strobe lights and tethered dogs.

Protective barriers. Experts agree the most effective control measures are physical barriers including wire cages for new growth and fences for established growth. Conventional deer-proof fences are made of woven wire. They should be at least 8 feet high. Electric fences are another possibility, particularly when marked with reflective tape.

These are exciting times in the world of hydrangeas. The popularity of hydrangeas is soaring, encouraging plant breeders to produce new varieties. It can be a challenge to keep up with all the new varieties offered to the public. In an attempt to clear up some of the possible confusion, the author has assembled information about several hydrangea series, most of which have been recently introduced. Learning what the plants in the series have in common may help you in your search for the perfect hydrangea variety for your garden.

Frequently the breeders focus on one quality such as varieties smaller than the normal range, reblooming hydrangeas, and bicolor blossoms. If more than one trait is associated with a series (e.g. compact + rebloomer), this is noted in the series' description.

As with any plant introductions some may perform brilliantly and others may be found wanting as many gardeners over a wide geographical distribution test them in home gardens. It will be interesting to see which new varieties are the stars that survive the test of time.

Space limitations dictated a selective list. The series and varieties noted below are widely available in the United States.

The Series
Abracadabra™
 Hydrangea Series
Cityline™ Series
Dutch Ladies™ Series
Edgy™ Hydrangea Series
Endless Summer® Collection
Forever & Ever® Series
Halo Hydrangeas™ Series
Kaleidoscope® Series
 (aka Hovaria® Series)
Let's Dance®
 Hydrangea Series
Royal Majestics® Series
Teller Series

Abracadabra™ Hydrangea Series, *Black satin stems,* developed by Katrin Meinl of Dresden, Germany.
Abracadabra™ Orb (mophead)
Abracadabra™ Star (lacecap)

Cityline™ Series. *Compact plants + large blooms*. This series was developed by Franz-Xaver and Konrad Rampp of Germany. Many other city names are included in the series but they are not currently available in the United States.
Cityline™ Berlin (mophead)
Cityline™ Paris (mophead)
Cityline™ Rio
 (bicolored mophead)
Cityline™ Venice (mophead)
Cityline™ Vienna (mophead)

Dutch Ladies™ Series. *Compact plants + large blooms.* This series was developed by Daan van der Spek, Netherlands, for the florist (cut flower) and potted plant trades so don't expect them to be particularly cold hardy. The varieties, with female names starting with the letter "S", include both mophead and lacecap forms.
Sabrina™ (bicolor mophead, white edged with rose)
Sandra™ (bicolor lacecap, white with a red edge)
Selina™ (lacecap)
Shakira™ (white mophead)
Sharona™ (bicolor mophead, pink with yellow centers)
Sheila™ (lacecap)
Sonja™ (mophead)
Soroya™ (white lacecap)
Stella™ (mophead)

Edgy™ Hydrangea Series. *Bicolored flowers*
Edgy™ Hearts (bicolored mophead developed by Katrin Meinl of Dresden, Germany)
Edgy™ Orbits (bicolored lacecap with double flowers developed by Tim Wood, Spring Meadow Nursery, U.S.)

Endless Summer® Collection. *Rebloomers*. Produced by Bailey Nurseries and Dr. Michael Dirr.
Endless Summer®
 The Original (mophead)
Endless Summer® 'Blushing Bride' (white mophead)
Twist-n-Shout® (lacecap)

Forever & Ever® Series. *Compact plants + rebloomers*. This series was introduced in 2005 with the first introduction called, simply, Forever & Ever Hydrangea. As other varieties were added to the series, the names started to become more descriptive. All are mopheads except for Forever & Ever® Summer Lace, a lacecap variety. The plants come from the Berry Family of Nurseries in the United States.

Forever & Ever® Blue Heaven
Forever & Ever® Double Pink
Forever & Ever® Fantasia
Forever & Ever® Hydrangea
Forever & Ever®
    Peace Hydrangea
    (double flowers)
Forever & Ever®
    Peppermint (bicolor)
Forever & Ever® Pistachio
Forever & Ever®
    Red Hydrangea
Forever & Ever®
    Summer Lace (lacecap)
Forever & Ever®
    Together (double flowers)
Forever & Ever® White Out

Halo Hydrangeas™ Series.
Bicolor flowers + compact plants. Introduced by Hines Horticulture.
Angel Eyes™ (mophead)
Angel Lace™ (lacecap)
Angel Robe™ (mophead)
Angel Smile™ (mophead)
Angel Song™ (mophead)
Angel Star™ (mophead)
Angel Wings™ (mophead)

Kaleidoscope® Series
(aka **Hovaria® Series**). *Color changes over time*. Developed by Koos and Wilko Hofstede, Netherlands.
'Hobella' (lacecap)
'Hobergine' (mophead)
'Holibel' (lacecap)
'Homigo' (mophead)
'Hopaline' (mophead)
'Hopcorn' (mophead)

Let's Dance® Hydrangea Series.
Rebloomers. Introduced by Proven Winners® ColorChoice® Plants.
Let's Dance® Big Easy
    (mophead)
Let's Dance® Moonlight
    (mophead)
Let's Dance® Starlight
    (lacecap)

Royal Majestics® Series.
Trustworthy garden performers.
Produced by McCorkle Nurseries and Dr. Michael Dirr.
Midnight Duchess® (lacecap
    with purple-black stems)
Mini Penny™ (compact
    reblooming mophead)
Princess Lace®
    (white lacecap)
Queen of Pearls®
    (white mophead)

The Teller Series. *Large lacecap blooms on sturdy stems*. An early series, the plants bred in Switzerland over two decades from the late 1960s to the late 1980s continue to be popular, some with home gardeners while many are used for the potted trade where they are valued for sturdy stems, bright colors, and large, flat flowerheads. They break dormancy early and are not particularly cold hardy but their beautiful plate-like flowers are highly valued. ("Teller" means "plate".) Exbury Gardens in the New Forest in England is building a collection of these hybrids where they line two sides of the Hydrangea Walk.

The varieties, all lacecaps and all named for European birds, were developed at The Federal Research Institute for Horticulture, Wädenswil, Switzerland.
'Blaumeise'
    (blue tit, titmouse, also
    known as Teller Blue)
'Eisvogel' (kingfisher)
'Fasan' (pheasant, also
    known as Teller Red)
'Kardinal' (cardinal)
'Libelle' (dragonfly, also
    known as Teller White)
'Möwe' (seagull)
'Nachtigall' (nightingale)
'Pfau' (peacock)
'Rotdrossel' (redwing)
'Rotkehlchen' (redbreast)
'Zaunkönig' (wren)

Series Summary

Color changes over time:
  Kaleidoscope® Series.
Compact Plants: Cityline™;
  Dutch Ladies™;
  Forever & Ever®;
  Halo Hydrangeas™.
Bicolor flowers: Edgy™;
  Halo Hydrangeas™.
Black stems: Abracadabra™.
Large blooms: Cityline™;
  Dutch Ladies™;
  The Teller Series.
Rebloomers:
  Endless Summer®;
  Forever & Ever®;
  Let's Dance®.
**Trustworthy garden
  performers**:
  Royal Majestics®.

Books

Dirr, Michael, *Hydrangeas for American Gardens*, Timber Press, 2004.
Church, Glyn, *Complete Hydrangeas*, Firefly Books, 2007.
Van Gelderen, C.J. and D.M., *Encyclopedia of Hydrangeas*, Timber Press, 2004.
Harrison, Joan, *Hydrangeas: Cape Cod and the Islands*, Schiffer Publishing Ltd., 2012.

General hydrangea information

www.hydrangeamania.com
www.hydrangeashydrangeas.com

Mail order sources for plants

Hydrangea Farm Nursery: www.hydrangeafarm.com
Hydrangeas Plus: www.hydrangeasplus.com
Joy Creek Nursery: www.joycreek.com
Wilkerson Mill Gardens: www.hydrangea.com

Hydrangea Societies

Georgia: The American Hydrangea Society, www.americanhydrangeasociety.org.
Massachusetts: Cape Cod Hydrangea Society,
      www.capecodhydrangeasociety.blogspot.com
Missouri: St. Louis Hydrangea Society, www.stlouishydrangeasociety.org.
South Carolina: CSRA Hydrangea Society, www.csrahydrangeasociety.org.
Tennessee: Mid-South Hydrangea Society, www.midsouthhydrangea.com.